The Complete
TROUT
AND
SALMON
Fisherman

The Complete
TROUT
AND
SALMON
Fisherman

Edited by Jack Thorndike

David & Charles
Newton Abbot   London   North Pomfret (Vt)   Vancouver

British Library Cataloguing in Publication Data

The complete trout and salmon fisherman.
1. Salmon-fishing 2. Trout fishing
I. Thorndike, Jack
799.1'7'55   SH684

ISBN 0-7153-7717-5

Library of Congress Catalog Card Number: 78-60987

Typeset by Northern Phototypesetting Company, Bolton
and printed in Great Britain
by Redwood Burn Limited, Trowbridge
for David & Charles (Publishers) Limited
Brunel House Newton Abbot Devon

Published in the United States of America
by David & Charles Inc
North Pomfret Vermont 05053 USA

Published in Canada
by Douglas David & Charles Limited
1875 Welch Street North Vancouver BC

Contents

Salmon

Sea-Trout

Flies

Introduction

Memories are made of fishing. Wherever and whenever anglers gather the conversation inevitably turns to days gone by—days recollected with pleasure, often ecstasy—as anglers recall, not always that occasion when the big one got away, but a triumph achieved when the odds were against them. The difficult fish that they are entitled to believe fell to their fly, either because they had chosen the right pattern or, more likely, because they presented it so correctly that no fish could refuse it.

Fly fishermen thrive on such nostalgic occasions. They delight in telling their stories, and their fellow fishers are equally absorbed as the tales unfold, reminding them of similar incidents of their own efforts to catch some elusive fish.

The articles in this book, likewise, will bring back memories, not just of good fish caught, but of varied fishing techniques developed and practised with success between July 1955, when *Trout and Salmon* was first published, and December 1976. This book spans that period.

In those years *Trout and Salmon* published well over three thousand articles covering every aspect of fishing with rod and line for trout, sea-trout and salmon. Some contributors were, and still are, household names in the world of game fishing. Sadly, some are not now with us. Others, not so well known, were equally expert in their own particular branch of the sport. All had practised before they preached and had something of value to say. *Trout and Salmon*, the only magazine devoted solely to angling for game fish, was, and still is, their medium.

And so, over these years under review, the magazine has printed a great variety of contributions. Many, because of their practical advice, aimed at making us more proficient fly fishermen. Others have helped to bring us a fish or two when the odds seemed set against us. Still more, in their wisdom, have helped to make fishing more enjoyable and rewarding.

After a careful study of the issues spanning these twenty-one years it is surprising how little we have changed in our fishing styles and methods, and in how we present a fly or bait for salmon. The techniques described in some of the earlier issues are the methods of today, albeit with some refinements.

In these years we have seen the development of stillwater trout fishing in our modern reservoirs and man-made lakes. Articles reveal the enthusiasm of followers of this style of fly fishing, eager to impart their views in the hope they will help others catch more fish.

Although methods, especially for the river fisherman, have changed little, the art of fishing has been made easier, and frequently more successful, by the great advances in tackle materials and design. Lightweight rods and reels, and a variety of plastic-coated lines have come on the market to make fishing less tiring and consequently more pleasurable.

Of necessity, the selection of articles published in this book has to be restricted, and so cannot hope to cater for all the many aspects of game fishing so comprehensively reported on in the 258 issues of *Trout and Salmon* under review. Nevertheless it has been made with care in the hope that readers will sit back, reflect and enjoy the writings of those who have had something pertinent to say about a sport that never fails to enthral us.

Jack Thorndike

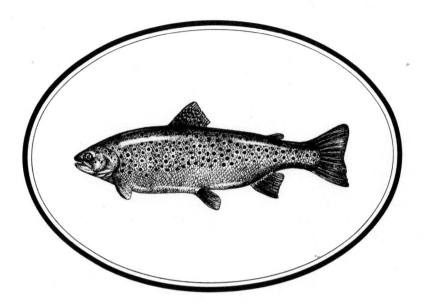

Trout

The Shasta-steelhead story

The water at the point where a tiny feeder entered the lake heaved and broke repeatedly as six big rainbow trout, splendid fish weighing between 3lb and 5lb, milled restlessly round at their spawning. As Alex Behrendt and I stood watching, I asked him whether all this effort and expenditure of energy would come to nothing. Alex began to explain that these were Shasta-type fish, that those of steelhead origin would not begin spawning for another month or so and that a small proportion of hatched fry might be produced.

As he spoke I began to realise how little I knew (and, I believe, the average fly fisherman knows) about these grand rainbows. The result was that I decided to write this article, which is based on the information given me by the owner of Two Lakes.

Rainbow trout (*Salmo irideus*) were introduced into this country from the Shasta Mountains area of California near the end of the nineteenth century. They came mainly from the Sacramento River and its tributary, the McCloud River. Their fighting qualities, their

11

willingness to rise to the dry fly freely and above all, their rate of growth—roughly twice that of our indigenous brown trout—soon commended them to fishery owners, trout farmers and fly fishermen. A rainbow boom began. One of the results was that the demand for the fertilised ova, which were imported for hatching, soon began to exceed the supplies available to the American exporters.

Thus it was that a situation was created, thanks once again to the cupidity of man, that was to have a profound and far-reaching effect on the future and on the reputation of rainbow trout in this country. Some unprincipled exporters of the spawn, anxious to fulfil valuable orders that they could not otherwise have met, dispatched consignments of steelhead ova in its place.

Naturally enough, none of the recipients noticed the difference. Unwitting breeders and owners of rivers or lakes carefully hatched out the spawn and successfully reared the fry, which grew into fine silvery young fish. These were then distributed or turned into local fisheries, in anticipation of the excellent sport they would provide in a season or so.

The inevitable, of course, happened. By the time they had reached their second year, those young steelheads that had not already been caught experienced that undeniable instinctive urge to return to the sea, which had for years prompted the migration of their American ancestors. Those placed in rivers moved off downstream. The only exceptions were the Derbyshire Wye, the Chess and the Misbourne, where the fish settled down, probably because they were unwilling to enter the rivers into which these tributaries flow.

Steelhead type

The fish of steelhead origin placed in stillwater headed for the outlets and, where they could find a way out, embarked on their journey towards salt water. Those whose exit was barred, congregated at the lower outlets of the lakes and lochs into which they had been introduced and restlessly swam back and forth, vainly searching for means by which to respond to their inbred desire for the ocean.

So it came about that a heavy black—but quite unjustified —mark was placed against the rainbow's reputation in this country. Countless clubs, associations and private owners must have stocked with what they thought were rainbows that mysteriously vanished without a trace. 'We've tried them once. Never again,' was a comment on the experiment that was heard all over England.

Another disadvantage that soon became apparent among those fish of steelhead origin that did not succeed in escaping was that in the spring they were prone either to become spawn-bound, with fatal consequences, or to sicken and eventually die after a fruitless shedding of their spawn.

Another black mark was awarded to the unfortunate rainbow. Further complications followed. The actual breeding of the true rainbow strain, by means of stripped fish, was successfully tried in this country and soon became widespread. Unhappily, as this developed, the rainbow and steelhead strains became inextricably mixed. Eventually, the Shasta rainbow itself fell victim to the massive rearing programme in the United States. The true, free-rising, dour-fighting Shasta is no more. Only fish sadly and loosely labelled as being of the Shasta type are now available.

It is, I think, generally known that the rainbow and the steelhead trout of the United States stand in the same relation to each other as our brown trout do to sea-trout. Steelheads, like sea-trout, make an annual migration to the sea. Rainbows, which live only for four or five years, and our brown trout do not.

Both Shasta rainbows and steelheads are commonly referred to as *Salmo irideus*, a name they were given because of the distinctive iridescent band on their flanks. Some authorities, however, support the view that they should more properly be known as *Salmo gairdneri*.

Just as the sea-trout and brown trout have characteristics that normally make it a simple matter to differentiate between them, so

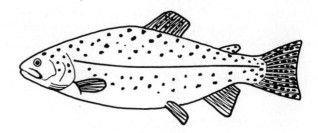

Shasta type

our rainbows with steelhead characteristics may be picked out from the Shasta type if one knows what to look for.

The main differences are that the steelhead type are February–April spawners, are covered with small black spots, which extend well below the lateral line, have a red band on the side that is not pronounced, and are more elongated in shape, generally with a larger head; the Shasta type are November–February spawners, are lighter in colour, with fewer spots, which are often thick on the tail although it is unusual to find any below the lateral line, have a clearly defined red band on the flanks and often have orange-red gill covers, their heads are smaller, often with a more developed neb, and the fish are deeper, commonly hump shaped.

Other American forms of *Salmo irideus* are comparable with our lake trout, such as Loch Leven fish and some Irish lake trout.

Recently there have been indications that time has come to the aid of the unfortunate rainbow. Years of breeding from fish that have become accustomed to English waters and conditions appear at last to have eradicated that upsetting desire to head seawards during the second year. Rainbows no longer congregate round stillwater outlets as they did only a few years ago. Instead, in the late autumn and early spring, they tend to become more preoccupied with spawning. The majority of them now succeed in ridding themselves of their spawn and sometimes a small proportion of this hatches out to provide a welcome bonus to fishery owners.

More important still, the parent fish are beginning to acquire a higher post-spawning recovery rate, so that a few of them have regained, or almost completely regained, condition by the time the following season opens. So it is that the circumstances of seventy or so years ago, which caused so much disappointment and trouble, have now begun to turn in our favour. Some of the fish of 5lb and more in weight, which would previously have died, now often survive the winter, to provide sport for the fisherman and to reduce to a small extent the restocking costs of fishery owners.

A permanent reminder of the disservice that that magnificent fish the steelhead unwittingly did to rainbow trout fishing in this country remains. Fish distinctly spotted below the lateral line bear such marking as an indication that they can count the steelhead among their ancestors. The spots remain, but the instinct to migrate at last seems to have forsaken them. Whether careful, selective breeding will ever eradicate the steelhead influence and produce fish that closely resemble the original Shastas remains to be seen. That it is within the realm of possibility is shown by the fact that in some countries work on these lines is already being done.

July 1970   *'Rags' Locke*

What makes a dry-fly fisherman?

I've just caught my first fish of 1960. I feel a renegade, however. This first fish was a salmon, and I am really a trout fisherman by nature. Yet here I am—on the Caragh River—running after bigger game. My excuse, of course, is that my trout fishing does not begin till May.

I fear that my trout-fishing friends will look at me suspiciously. They will accuse me of forsaking my first love. My salmon-fishing friends will think I have joined them. One of them has already written: 'I see you're taking up a worthwhile sport at last.' I must disillusion him.

What a thrill that salmon was! What a marvellous river this is! But I shall always be a trout fisherman at heart even though I may have a few lapses from grace.

Probably my main reason is that I am not at all a patient person. I do like excitement. On this lovely Irish river, at this time of the year, there should be no lack of it. When the salmon come in from the sea, silver and strong, almost every cast should cover one of them. While one's fly (or bait) is in the water, one's heart is in one's mouth.

But I shall not always be lucky enough to fish water such as this. On other salmon water I have been frankly bored. I have found myself casting in a sort of numb rhythm, repeating to myself, 'I came here to fish and I'm jolly well going to fish, whether there's a chance of catching anything or not'. I know that this is a bad way to fish, but I have not been able to avoid it.

Dry-fly fishing for trout on the other hand, needs no patience at all. It is never, never repetitive. Patience! One is so tired of hearing the word from people who have never cast a fly. Dry-fly fishing is desperately thrilling. That is why you find strong men quivering with fear behind a bush, in case a half-pound trout should see them.

What really makes a dry-fly fisherman? In this article I should like to enquire for a change—not into the nature of trout and flies—but into the nature of fly fishermen, especially dry-fly fishermen. What qualities do they have?

To start with, dry-fly fishermen must be a little mad. Everyone seems to think so and everyone is probably right. We go to incredible trouble to catch a very small fish. Unlike a salmon, it has no commercial value. Yet we make a great fuss about it. Our wives, after some coaxing, consent to cook it, and will occasionally eat it so as not to offend us.

There is, however, a good deal of method in our madness. Most of the really good dry-fly fishermen I know are extremely methodical men. They are the sort of men who enjoy working out a way of tackling a problem, and then applying their method step by step, until it is solved. On the whole, they do not enjoy short cuts.

It is easy to see why they succeed in catching trout on a dry fly. Here, short cuts are more often fatal than not. If we leave out any step—such as choosing the right fly or approaching a trout carefully—we are liable to bungle the whole business.

A dry-fly fisherman must be an inquisitive person. When he sees a trout behaving in a special way, he must always ask 'Why?' Unless he is constantly asking 'why?' he will not catch many fish. When a trout refuses him, he must look for a reason.

Again, he must watch everything that goes on around him, particularly the insects. If he is not inquisitive about insects, as well as trout, he will miss a lot of interest, and a lot of sport.

On the whole, I do not think salmon fishermen exercise nearly so much curiosity. Good salmon fishermen do and know much about the habits of salmon. But too many are content just to go to the water with a fixed-spool reel, without knowing much about their quarry. If the water is right, they can pull out a salmon or two. Why should they learn?

Curiosity by itself will help nearly anyone to become a good dry-fly fisherman. But if such a man has powers of logic as well—if he is good at relating cause and effect—he will become a first-class trout fisherman, not just a good one.

More than that, he may find new ways to catch trout. He may evolve new techniques. Goodness knows, there are plenty of new things to be found out in trout fishing. Most innovations are arrived at by a combination of curiosity, observation and logic.

Skues was a logical man. He was a lawyer. In describing the beginning of his nymph-fishing experiments, he wrote: 'I found that there were occasions when the winged wet fly, cast upstream to feeding fish, was quite efficacious ... it was a long time before I realised that these occasions occurred nearly always when the trout were nymphing and not taking the natural fly.'

Once he realised this—once he adduced the right cause to the right effect—nothing could stop the development of nymph fishing. One of the things I like about dry-fly fishermen is that you often hear them say: 'I'm going to try out a new theory today.' How much more fun it is to fish when one is trying out a new theory of one's own, rather than merely applying other people's!

I believe that good dry-fly fishing is really an attitude of mind. Manual dexterity plays little part in it. Admittedly, it is a lovely sight to see a really good caster. We may envy those gifted individuals who can cast into a wind without effort or throw a 'shepherd's crook' at will. But these skills are not a major part of the sport.

To me, the biggest appeal of dry-fly fishing is the constant interest that it has, from day to day, and from moment to moment. One could never call it a 'contemplative man's recreation', if what the old phrase means is that you can sit on a bank and think of something else while you are fishing.

This may be true of some forms of fishing—but not of dry-fly fishing. It is all absorbing. It requires constant attention, constant vigilance, constant brain-work. Every trout is a separate problem and must be treated as such. The only thing you can think about when you are dry-fly fishing is dry-fly fishing!

One cannot be surprised that dry-fly fishing is becoming more and more popular. I am not suggesting that it is in any way better than wet-fly fishing. These two forms of trout fishing are, in my opinion, the two best sports in the world, and the best fisherman is probably the man who can change from one to the other, as conditions demand.

May 1960   *Dermot Wilson*

The slob trout

Most of our game fishes are talked and written about extensively but the slob or estuarine trout gets only an occasional mention. He is, of course, met with less frequently and this may be the reason for his being neglected. These trout are not encountered in every river or estuary and I have no idea why he should prefer one estuary to another.

Let us first consider his name—slob or estuarine. I think that slob is the better, it fits his character better, both as a fighter and for the table. As a fighter he is apt to be lethargic and only his bulk prolongs the contest after he is hooked. Estuarine may be a name that fits his chosen home, but in every other way it is, I think, misleading.

My dictionary tells me that slob refers to mud or mire, to a clumsy or dull person or one whose personality is offensive. I think this is a little unfair; estuaries may be muddy, but so are some rivers that hold trout, and I do not find these fish offensive—merely rather dull.

Just what is a slob trout? It has been suggested that it is a brown trout that has acquired the habit of living in an estuary. This sounds reasonable and if we accept this explanation we can but suppose that the slob trout finds that the estuary provides better food and better quarters than the seasonal austerity of the river. But I wonder if this is the right answer. We are told that a sea-trout is merely a brown trout that has taken to migratory habits. It is unlikely that this metamorphosis took place suddenly, indeed it is much more likely that it took generations to accomplish this change. Is it possible that the slob trout is still an example of this change of habit and that the future generations of the present slob trout may in the end produce sea-trout? Nature seldom works hurriedly. I have a vague feeling that this might prove to be the answer.

The habits of the slob trout are widely different from the migratory and the non-migratory species. But first there must be an estuary; rivers without such an outlet do not have these fish. Rivers that have lochs or deep stillwater reaches subject to tidal action nearly always do. It is reasonable to suppose that slob trout find that their metabolism can accept the brackish conditions. But they could not tolerate it if the change in salinity was too sudden. The food of the estuary, for the same reason, is more akin and more suitable to the gentle change that survival demands. But this food appears to lack something, unless we have to assume that it is all used to bring about the change to a full migratory habit.

Let us admit that slob trout are not the most sporting of fish. They do grow big and this bulk may give a false sense of strength, but it is the mass rather than fighting instinct that is deceptive.

I have caught a few of these slob trout both at home and in Iceland. The Icelandic ones are better fighters; this may be due to the colder waters of a sub-arctic island and possibly to a different form of food. Icelandic estuaries are seldom muddy, they are mostly paved with gravel, sand or lava. So the smaller crustaceans are those that like this kind of bottom and are also those that provide greater vigour in the fish that eat them.

In my own river on the west coast of Scotland we have an estuary and there are a few slob trout in it. These fish are never found above the tide-affected reaches. They average about 3lb in weight, they spawn low down in the burns that feed the estuary and they stay only a day or so to complete the act. There may be many more of these slob trout than I imagine in the estuary because it is not fished, indeed much of its waters are out of reach of any angler without a boat and there is no temptation to fish its wider reaches. So it is only an accident when a slob trout is caught. They take readily enough when they are in those parts of the lower river that are fished. But most of them I know of have been caught by younger anglers using worms. I am not suggesting that a worm is the best bait for slob trout, but I imagine that he would favour a worm before he would a fly.

I said before that they grow big and the famous Orkney trout from Loch Stenness is an undoubted example of the species—it weighed 29lb.

In Iceland I have caught a number of these fish. These Icelandic slob trout have the same limited range. They are not caught above tide-affected waters. But they are better fighters and better eating. The few I have caught have varied in size between 3lb and 8lb, and there is no doubt that I have not caught the largest of them. As at home, these Icelandic slob trout extend beyond the range of anglers as they are occasionally caught in the nets far outside the river beats and in water that is more saline than in my estuary at home. Yet they have the same distinctive yellow colouring and the red spots of the true brown trout. Again in Iceland the percentage of cocks to hens is higher. I can think of no reason for this. But it is only fair to state that the numbers I have caught or seen are too few for me to be dogmatic about them.

The slob trout may be a rather dull fish, but there is the possibility that he may be one of the most interesting of all our fishes, in that we are witnessing a process of evolution and up till now have not realised this fact. If my vague surmise should be correct, then I consider that the slob trout is a very valuable fish.

April 1960   *R N Stewart*

Where Skues 'found' the nymph

It is difficult to imagine any place on earth so steeped in the greatest traditions of dry-fly and nymph fishing as the Abbot's Barton water on the Itchen, a mile or so from Winchester Cathedral, where Izaak Walton takes his rest. The chimes echo across the meadows today as they did when F M Halford, J W Hills, William Senior and the rest plied their gentle art upon these classic waters.

G S Marryat and Francis Francis held the tenancy here until 1883, when it was taken on by Mr Irwin Cox, at that time joint proprietor of *The Field*, and it was Cox who introduced a guest to the water, a courteous man, yet forthright, with poor eyesight and damaged wrists, who immediately fell in love with Abbot's Barton. Little did the guest realise at that time that he was to fish here for an incredible fifty-six years before resigning his membership, partly to save further embarrassment to his fellows by his highly successful use of the submerged fly, and partly because of the introduction of stock fish, which in his view was undesirable.

Of course, this little wizard of the Itchen was none other than the great G E M Skues, who refused to accept that the dry fly was the only successful means or the only sporting method, although he did for some years use only the floating fly, influenced by the doctrines of a creed laid down by the mighty prophets; doctrines that, even today, are followed by many who fish on waters that lend themselves to the exclusive use of the dry fly, and by those who enjoy this method above all else. He attended those nightly gatherings in Halford's rooms at a Winchester hotel, where the problems of fly fishing were analysed, techniques discussed, and where many of the principles of the dry fly were formed.

Skues came upon the truth by chance, when one day on the Itchen his fly became submerged and he discovered on the retrieve that he was into a fish. The trout was lost, but this incident was to mark the beginnings of nymph fishing as we know it today. An enquiring mind, coupled with persistence, great courage and literary genius, gave the angling world a new dimension to the sport. At his death, nymph fishing was still frowned upon by many, but his words live on, and further developments of the technique by Sawyer and Kite have now established the use of nymphs as a wholly acceptable supplement to the dry fly.

For some years I had longed to visit Abbot's Barton, if only to walk in the footsteps of those who had gone before and cast my fly in hallowed places. Imagine my delight when I received two tickets from Roy Darlington, who now leases the water with his brother, Ronald. I had to book my days in advance, for the number of rods here is strictly limited, and rightly so.

Trout are not uppermost in the thoughts of the visitor as he approaches the water, for this is a place where he wishes simply to look about and savour the atmosphere. Over to the right a fishing hut nestles among the trees 100yd or so from the site of the original *Piscatoribus Sacrum*, where so many great anglers gathered to enjoy a rest, and perhaps a glass or two, when the trout were not feeding.

There are carriers everywhere, seemingly running in all directions. Some chuckle swiftly over clean gravel and through bright water plants; others glide quietly, nearly at bank height, allowing the angler to cast from several yards back in the meadow. But for me the greatest charm of this historic fishery is the sight of the multitude of little footbridges that remain unaltered, save for repairs, and that feature so often in the minor tactics so delightfully described by Skues. Indeed, one can recognise some of these today, so vivid are the pictures he left upon the minds of fishermen.

One such is the ancient bridge that spans the Five Hatches stretch, in the middle of the fishery, over which the hay carts passed on their journey across the meadows. There was hay thick upon the bridge this day, and it enabled me to catch a trout rising beneath.

The bridge is about 3ft above the water and 3–4yd broad. Casting underneath was quite out of the question and it was not possible to float a fly from above because of the presence of a fair-sized bush. Getting below, I cast a long slack line over the top of the bridge and to my delight the fly fell right and without drag. The fish rose as if it meant it, but I had failed to allow for the fact that I was pulling the fly away by striking.

Thanks to the hay on the bridge my fly did not catch in the woodwork on the retrieve, and three times more I was lucky. At the fifth cast his troutship took and was on, and was kind enough to remain beneath the bridge, allowing me time to clamber on to the rickety structure and net him out from there. The snipe were drumming in the heavens and the lapwings wheeled and screeched in warning, but somewhere, close at hand, I felt sure I heard a quiet word of approval.

Down on the Park Stream, by Duck's Nest Spinney, Skues fished mostly from the right bank with the trees close behind. Here he perfected his 'switch' to the fish lying alongside the tussocks on the far side, and I remembered well that he found them especially shy when approached from the left bank. I could see the spot from which he must have cast, but foolishly I did not cross over as he advised. The tussocks are there today, and the trout still know 'what tussocks are for'. I am ashamed to say that I put them down one after another as I approached. Next time I will heed those words of wisdom.

At the bottom of the Barton carrier, a lovely length of stickles and quiet pools, two good fish were feeding steadily a yard or so apart. The first, although taking naturals well enough, was not in the least impressed by my imitations. He looked at them, but appeared gut shy and sheered off at the slightest suggestion of drag. A change to Black Gnat and a fluky cast did the trick, and he fairly shot upstream, making the reel sing its merry tune. Then, turning, he came down past me like a rocket and thrashed about under the bridge below. Winding in slack line furiously, I managed to gain control and netted a beautiful fat trout of 1lb 10oz. The second fish had gone down, but I saw him later and put him at close on 3lb. My five fish on this first visit to Abbot's Barton averaged 1lb apiece, which I thought was respectable enough.

All these fish, including the four that were returned, came from the carriers that form the major part of this fishery, and although I saw a few heavy trout in the main Itchen, I found them shy and selective. This is big-fish water, running deep and steady, and it is easy to imagine the existence here of trout weighing 5lb and more. Indeed, I am told that electric fishing has shown up fish of almost twice this weight. They seldom rise, of course, but on a summer's night when the sedges scutter and blue-winged olives flutter gracefully on the stream, who knows?

The carriers provide good spawning areas, but sufficient fish are introduced to supplement the native stocks. Rainbows and brown trout are turned in, and anyone visiting the water on a day ticket should find plenty of rising fish, but a most careful approach is necessary here; fly pattern can be of major importance and precise presentation can be vital.

Sadly, the city of Winchester creeps ever closer to this sacred place. To the west a new housing development is springing up along the road to King's Worthy and down towards Chalkpit Cottage, but as yet it is hidden behind the trees. Over to the east, across the main river, a large factory booms a metallic strain upon the ear and ahead a flyover carries traffic across the meadows alongside Jenny's Creek, which Skues called the Highland Burn.

Yet as he walks through these lush water-meadows, gay with all the flowers of the marsh, and here and there a spinney, the angler is glad that this shrine is as yet untouched by those who know not of its glorious past. He may yet savour this piece of old England, but he is aware that some may have designs upon this land, and may one day wish to tear down those beloved footbridges and fill in the ancient watercourses. I shudder at the thought. Abbot's Barton is a priceless jewel at the heart of fly-fishing traditions. It must, at all costs, be preserved.

October 1975   *Gordon Mackie*

When entomology does count

More than once in recent issues of *Trout and Salmon* writers have asked the question: 'How much knowledge of entomology must you have to be a fairly successful fly fisher?' The answer, as far as chalk-stream fishing is concerned, is that you can be quite successful in terms of being able to catch trout and grayling without knowing much about entomology at all.

A competent caster, equipped with a reliable dry fly and an effective nymph pattern, and skilled in the practical handling of both, may hope to be successful most days throughout the chalk-stream season even if his knowledge of entomology amounts to little. I have taught reasonably competent casters to attain this standard inside a season. It amounted largely to persuading them to recognise whether fish were feeding on or beneath the surface and to present their artificial accordingly.

The most important requirement for the chalk-stream fly fisher, as far as entomology is concerned, is to have an elementary understanding of the main stages through which upwinged flies pass during their metamorphosis: larva, nymph, dun, spinner and spent female. If the angler is aware which stage of the fly is featuring prominently in the fish's diet at a given time, he can offer it at least an approximate imitation of what it is expecting to see and thereby enjoy a reasonable chance of deceiving it.

The importance of individual patterns is often much overrated. There are times when pattern matters, but what matters much more is knowing whether to fish on, in, just beneath, below or well below the surface film. However much entomology you may know, unless you use your eyes to guide your tactics, you are unlikely to be consistently successful.

You can even catch fish successfully on the dry fly alone provided you offer your artificial only to those seen to be feeding on the surface. Some nymphing fish will take a dry fly but many will not. If this sounds simple, elementary and logical, I am glad, because chalk-stream fly fishing is all these things, most of the time.

A number of fly fishers of my acquaintance, now well on in years, have discovered in their old age that they can catch pretty well as many fish on, say, one or two patterns of dry flies, as they used to take on a variety of artificials when their eyesight was keener and changing a fly had not become a tiresome fatigue. One octogenarian friend still does well using nothing but the Orange Quill, and a well-known upper Avon master nowadays takes two-thirds of his fish on a rough-looking Black Gnat and one-third on a Ginger Quill. But these are experienced fly fishers. When trout are taking nymphs they do not bombard them with their favourite dry-fly patterns and then blame these for their want of success.

At least half the battle in chalk-stream trouting is concealing from the fish the fact that they are being fished for. I notice, time and again, that rods who fail on hard-flogged association water most often do so because they ignore this simple rule. Remember, always, the sound military principle of achieving surprise!

There are a few occasions most seasons when trout elect to feed mainly on some specific insect, in some particular stage of its metamorphosis. The fish, being in a set frame of mind, can then be taken with certainty only when offered something that passes their scrutiny as being a representation broadly similar to the natural on which they are feeding with such single-minded concentration.

Four such circumstances are of sufficient significance, most years, to warrant individual discussion although even these rarely occur more than three or four times a season on any one chalk-stream. Let us consider them in chronological order of occurrence.

First of course, come the falls of land-bred black flies, which occur most years during the opening days of the chalk-stream trout season. The flies concerned are the hawthorn fly, *Bibio marci*, and the black gnat, *Dilophus febrilis*. After a mild winter, especially, these flies may be blown on to the water in tremendous numbers at the end of April and the beginning of May.

Trout are more fond of these insects than of any others of which I have knowledge. The hawthorn, being the larger, is the one they prefer and the one they watch for. The artificial hawthorn is the pattern with which the discerning fly fisher hopes to take a limit basket on the first morning of the season. Others knowing nothing of the hawthorn may still hope to pick up a brace or two during the olive hatch using any one of a variety of dun patterns, and still count themselves successful. How do you judge success?

Next comes the mayfly—at least on some chalk-streams. When trout really settle to eat these large insects, as they may on two or three days during the hatch or sometimes in the evening during a fall of spent gnat, they haven't much time for other flies, natural or artificial. But even then you can generally find the exception. And my old friend who sticks to the Black Gnat still catches his share of trout on this unlikely artificial at mayfly time!

It is in the evening from midsummer onwards for a few weeks, that trout tend to be most finicky on the chalk-streams. The two most likely causes of this behaviour, as far as surface feeders are concerned, are evening hatches of pale watery duns and dusk hatches of pale evening duns.

The pale watery dun (*Bibioculatus*) hatches well on these rivers on most June days but is, to a large extent, ignored by trout in the quick-hatching dun stage, although they take the nymph. But when this dun elects to hatch in the evening in summer, it seems then to sit a little longer on its shuck. Thus it becomes easier and more rewarding prey to indolent trout than when it hatches with rapidity in the noonday sunshine.

When trout do settle to feed on pale watery duns in the evening, they tend to ignore reliable spinner patterns, like the pheasant tail Red Spinner, with which they can usually be taken on most evenings from June onwards. The fly fisher with a rudimentary knowledge of entomology should be quick to diagnose the reason for such refusals, and to counter them effectively with his pale watery patterns.

The pale evening dun (*Procloëon pseudorufulum*) is a small whitish olive, which at times hatches freely from the slower flowing reaches of the chalk-streams and many rivers elsewhere in these islands. These hatches usually occur at dusk, quite often at the same time as the familiar dusk hatches of blue-winged olives, on warm evenings from mid-summer to about the end of August. On these occasions, trout usually elect to take the tinier pale duns and unless you employ a suitably dressed artificial, like the pale evening dun, you cannot induce them to take.

Failure to detect and act on this well-established preference leads some fly fishers, brought up on Orange Quills and the like, to persuade themselves that trout feeding on blue-winged olive duns are not easy to catch. They are. But if trout are feeding on pale evening duns, it may be impossible to catch them without a suitable whitish artificial.

In these four situations, some knowledge of elementary entomology, in terms of identifying certain individual species or types of fly, is undoubtedly advantageous. Even in these cases, however, an acute observer to whom the scientific names of these flies are quite unknown, should still be able to connect what he sees trout eating with the kind of artificial he should tie on to give himself a reasonable chance of deceiving them.

I have found in practice that most acute observers are men with questing, inquiring minds who do not, for long, deny themselves the elementary knowledge so readily available nowadays.

Finally, there are various other occasions when some difficulty may be encountered. Among these may be mentioned heavy spring hatches of grannom in a few places, a sunrise flush of broadwings in July, a fall of ants in August, such as occurred on the middle Test in 1961, or an unusually heavy fall of male spurwing spinners in the autumn. In all these cases, if the fly fisher will just use his eyes, he is half-way to taking his fish.

February 1962   *Oliver Kite*

Enigmas of the lure

The dictionary definition of the term 'lure' is not of much help in an angling context, but to define it in our sense is rather difficult. However, to most anglers, a lure is a device that makes no attempt to imitate any kind of insect; that is usually from $1\frac{1}{2}$in to as much as 4in long; that has a 'wing' of hair or feather making a relatively small angle with the shank or shanks of the hook or hooks on which it is dressed; and that can be expected to arouse the disapproval of at least 25 per cent of fly fishers.

That is somewhat surprising, since the lure as we know it today is by no means new. Multi-hook lures were in use at Blagdon about seventy years ago, and were probably employed for sea-trout fishing a good deal earlier than that.

Why do trout take lures? I suggest that there may be three motives: hunger, curiosity, and aggression. It is important to distinguish these, because lures of different types are involved.

Not only trout, but also pike and perch attack lures, and it is significant that those lures that attract perch and pike best, are those that attempt to imitate small fish. The best lure I know of for catching perch is called the Hanningfield Lure. It incorporates features intended to suggest those of small perch or rudd: a speckled feather wing to suggest a scaly back; white hair underwing, with silver-ribbed body, to imitate the sides and belly; orange throat hackle and tail, to imitate fins; and a fish shape when drawn through the water.

This pattern is not generally effective for trout; it does well only when they are attacking concentrations of small coarse fish. One may speculate from this and from other evidence that when trout are eating small fish, a lure that incorporates some of the recognition features of small fish is the best choice; but when the trout are eating insects, daphnia or snails, a fish-imitating lure is by no means necessarily the best kind to offer them.

At this point the reader may ask, why use a lure when the fish are eating insects? Why not use an imitation of the insect species they are eating? I can only reply, why indeed? The fact is that we now have a section of trout fishers who constantly seek the short cut; they have no wish to involve themselves in the intellectual exercise of identifying the diet of the trout at a particular time and fishing, perhaps even devising, an imitation of that diet. They have found that they can avoid any need to do so by using a lure of some kind and pulling it fast through the area in which the trout are feeding. My role here is to report rather than to recommend, and I have therefore

Rainbow trout

to say that it would seem that the best sort of lure to use in such circumstances is one in which there are relatively few points of resemblance to small fish, but rather a general impression that is likely to attract most attention.

Among the ingredients that help in this are hot-orange hair, hackles or marabou; black, yellow and white materials, including fluorescent ones; and relatively fast movement. It seems possible that such lures, which include patterns such as the Whisky Fly, Chief Needabeh, Black Lure, Sweeney Todd and Yellow Peril, excite trout to attack them because their intrusion into a feeding territory is resented, or else they stimulate curiosity on the part of the trout.

We often find trout following such lures without taking them or, sometimes, plucking at them without being hooked. Since trout can swim much faster than any angler can retrieve a lure, such behaviour is surely evidence that the trout are either trying to drive away an intruder or are curious about the lure and wish to know what it feels like as well as what it looks like. A firm take in such circumstances is more likely to be due to the trout carrying aggression or curiosity to an extreme, rather than a desire to eat the lure. It may also be significant that a trout that has followed a lure, and has perhaps plucked at it, will seldom show interest if the same lure is offered to it a second time. This is perhaps evidence of curiosity rather than aggression.

For this reason, continuing to fish the same lure in the same area for long periods without success is unwise. All the trout within casting range will probably have examined the lure and lost interest in it during the first ten or fifteen minutes, and only a fish moving into the area and seeing the lure for the first time is likely to take. It therefore pays to change either the lure or one's place of fishing if no results are obtained within a quarter of an hour or so.

How should lures be constructed? This question brings us back to the trout's motivation. When the trout takes the lure for a little fish he means to eat, he attacks the head end, swimming parallel to the lure and turning quickly across its path. A single hook suffices, and the trout is usually firmly hooked in the scissors.

This will also happen when aggression or curiosity lead the trout to take a firm hold; but if not, then the chances of hooking a trout are increased if a hook is located at the rear of the lure, in a tandem arrangement of two or three hooks. Incidentally, perch attack a lure—or a real fish—quite differently from trout. They snap at the tail of their quarry, so if you want to catch a perch, put a hook right at the back of your lure and embellish it with hair or feather to imitate a tail quite positively.

How should lures be fished? Where trout are attacking concentrations of coarse-fish fry, use a fish-imitating lure and fish it slowly, trying different combinations of slow, steady pulls, little jerks and long pauses.

If you fish attention-attracting lures rather than fish-imitating ones, more often than not a steady, fast retrieve proves most effective; no pauses, no slowing down or speeding up. It so often happens that a trout takes a lure when an angler is reeling in his line, often after he has made cast after cast in the same area, that I am forced to conclude that the retrieve at constant speed has special attraction. Much the same applies when lures are trailed behind a moving boat, or where the same effect is obtained without flouting anti-trailing rules, by the use of lee-boards or special rudders.

Retrieving by reeling in involves loss of time, since a good deal of line has to be pulled off the reel and worked out after each retrieve. That can be avoided by tucking the rod under the arm and using both hands to pull the line through the butt ring, using a hand-over-hand motion to keep the lure moving at a constant speed. A smart tug with the hand will hook most of the taking fish.

This pre-supposes that the trout cannot be seen. Where they can, or where at least a bow wave made by a following trout is visible, it sometimes pays to stop the retrieve quite suddenly, pause, and start again equally suddenly, when the trout will often be found hooked.

It is also wise to remember that when using a fast-sinking line, a lure is being pulled by the sinking line even though the angler is not retrieving. Takes quite often come at this time and unless the angler is alert to their possibility, many will be missed. When this happens it is a clear hint to allow less sinking time; to start the retrieve sooner after casting, because the trout aren't as deep as you thought!

There is a great deal of debate about the ethics of lure-fishing. I should be sorry to see any restrictions placed on it in large water-supply reservoirs and other sheets of water of comparable size, where there is no evidence that its use leads to too high a catch rate. When trout are eating fry, or when they are obviously not feeding on insects, the use of an appropriate lure may catch a fish or two and

save an angler, who may have travelled a long way, from a blank
day. In these conditions, using a lure is perfectly reasonable.

I am, however, sorry for those anglers who have no ideas beyond
casting out a lure as far as possible and stripping it in as fast as they
can, regardless of what the trout are doing. They don't know how
much pleasure they are missing. That they often catch a lot of fish is
undeniable, but they never learn what fly fishing is really about.

July 1975   *Richard Walker*

The nymph in stillwater

Nymph fishing is developing fast among lake and reservoir
fishermen, but there is still a good deal of uncertainty about its
methods and techniques. I had a letter the other day from a man who
said he had caught scores of trout on a nymph at distances of 30yd
or more, and I think he was hurt when I said I did not think that was
nymph fishing, even though he was fishing a nymph pattern.

So let me explain the basic method and techniques as pioneered by
Phillips and Bell more than half a century ago and developed since
then by many skilful nymph fishermen who prefer it to the lure or wet
fly, not because it catches more fish (though sometimes it does), but
simply because of its attractions as a method of fishing.

A nymph fisherman who comes to it from fishing lures or wet fly
has to train himself to forget and avoid much of what he has
previously learned. He avoids long-distance casting, shooting-heads,
forward-tapers, heavy sinking lines, large flies, stripping-in and deep
wading. He can no longer fish in company, wading out thigh deep
and staking his position with a net.

Instead, he has to equip himself with the lightest possible rod, not
longer than 8ft 6in, and a double-tapered line, either silk or a floating
plastic line, which should never be heavier than AFTM 5 or 6. He
will use a long leader of 12ft or more, and a single nymph on a point
of 4–5lb breaking strain even in waters where he may expect to catch
a ten-pounder. That is the first difference. His tackle is much lighter

and more delicate, and he will not normally expect to cast more than 10–20yd at the outside. The reason for this is in the way the trout takes the nymph and in his method of fishing.

He will walk the banks, seeking small isolated bays and calm or comparatively calm water, which will allow him to locate underwater weed-beds—the feeding grounds—and to see the humps and whorls on the surface that indicate trout movement. When he finds an area where the trout are moving, he will try to keep himself out of sight, either by kneeling, keeping back from the edge or taking advantage of whatever cover there may be. Trout feeding in the margins are easily alarmed by movement and vibrations on the bank. Even the splash of a heavy line on the water disturbs them.

Having got into position, the fisherman puts his nymph within reach of the fish, which is more easily said than done. This is where presentation and watercraft are all important, and why long leaders are essential and why many nymph fishermen use silk in preference to plastic lines. Delicacy in presentation is the first priority.

Once the nymph is cast to the area where the trout are moving, it is allowed to sink. The nymph is lightly weighted under the thorax and often trout will take a nymph 'on the sink'. After it has sunk to a reasonable depth (and this is a matter for judgement), a slow retrieve is begun with an occasional induced take. It is difficult to say how slow the retrieve should be but, as a rough guide, a retrieve in dead calm water is too fast if line-wake forms on either the line or on the butt of the leader.

During the retrieve, the fisherman keeps his rod point low on the water to avoid line slack and pointed directly at the nymph. This is not to feel the take when it comes, but to obtain a cushion effect on the strike. He will rarely, if ever, feel a take. Trout feeding naturally on easily obtained food do not waste energy. The take is gentle and indicated only by a slight movement on the leader or line. Sometimes there's a twitch, sometimes the leader seems to 'go dead' during the retrieve. That is all. The strike must be quick but gentle—very quick and very gentle.

This, in general terms, is the method most nymph fishermen use, though there are, of course, many variations and refinements. But what patterns of fly do they use? These vary from exact imitations of the pond and lake olive nymphs to patterns that have the basic nymphal shape but can also suggest other insects, such as sedge pupae. It is a matter of personal preference, taste, opinion and experiment. The basic essential is to fish a pattern that imitates or suggests the natural food on which trout feed in the margins.

Most fishermen tie their own patterns, weighting them in the way that fits in best with the way they fish and the conditions of the water in which they are fishing. This is why, on the whole, nymph patterns available in the shops are not always satisfactory. My own personal belief is that provided the overall suggestion is of a natural insect, the colour or colours of the dressing may be much less important than the size of the hook. The trout must think he is taking natural food. The size and colour of the fly conform to that principle.

Well, that is nymph fishing. What are the advantages and disadvantages compared with other methods? One can argue about this for hours. Indeed, one does. Ultimately it must be a matter of personal preference. I like nymph fishing simply and solely because I find it more exciting and interesting. I know what I am doing or what I am trying to do. I don't have to worry about what flies to use. I use one pattern all the time, merely changing the size.

There is one disadvantage that should be mentioned. In rough water on big reservoirs it is difficult to see the takes. There are ways of dealing with this—for example, a big bushy palmer as a floating dropper which registers a take. But now we are going down to details. In general terms, since going over from lure and wet-fly fishing to the nymph, I have not found any overwhelming disadvantage in doing so. I have found fishing much more interesting and on the whole I like to think that I have caught more fish.

To sum up, briefly, one cannot do better than to quote from Frank Sawyer's book *Nymphs and The Trout*: 'Fishing a nymph or a bug in lakes and reservoirs is much the same as fishing these artificials in the slow-running reaches of a river. The key to success is in knowing just when a fish has taken and it is here I know many anglers fail. So many fish with nymphs and expect to get a pull or a snatch from their quarry, in much the same way as one does when fishing wet flies or lures. But the technique is different. If a nymph is fished properly, by this I mean in a way a fish expects a natural nymph to behave, the take of a fish is seldom registered on the rod. For nymphs to be really effective they have to be fished slowly.'

November 1975   *Conrad Voss Bark*

Limitations of purism in fly fishing

If I am a purist, and I would confess to being one only for personal enjoyment, I have to admit at the same time that I am also a sort of free-thinker so far as angling is concerned. A man who adheres to a particular technique because his neighbour has a fetish about it has decided to put convention above intelligence. There are many people who pay lip service to techniques and wish that they could free themselves of restriction. Not only is this so among dilettante trout fishermen, but also among salmon anglers who have a strange prejudice about the fly's superiority over spinner, sprat or shrimp. It doesn't demonstrate superior skill to fish a fly when fish won't look at the fly, but to persist certainly indicates a strange obsession with ritual.

One can hardly imply that purism is as common among salmon anglers as among members of exclusive fly-fishing clubs. Among those on the fringe, the everyday fly fisherman who goes to the streams and lakes outside the chalk-stream country, purism has come to mean either eccentricity or downright stuffiness. A purist is the sort of person who insists on making the simple difficult or the difficult next to impossible. He is a sort of Colonel Blimp, harmless and tolerated because his self-imposed rule leaves more fish for those less obsessed with ritual.

There are I think, two ends of the scale so far as the ordinary fly fisherman is concerned. With an ill-concealed smile he acknowledges the dry-fly enthusiast as the natural descendant of the Victorian chalk-stream angler. At the other end he refers to an angler known as the 'upstream wormer'. For this method too, has a certain mystery, since the worm is cast as far upstream as can be reasonably contrived and takes the trout as it comes trundling back. This is superior to standing on the bank with the worm trailing in the current while the angler falls into a daydream and waits for a tug. Upstream worming, like dry-fly purism, owes much to the great angling writers who gave one method respectability and the other the distinction of being called the ultimate in finesse.

No one can deny that it takes skill to handle a worm coming back down the water, through ripple and riffle, across shallow pools and over minor cascades, where, in the shelter of boulders or submerged stones, good trout may lie. The man who can do this, on those occasions when this technique alone may be productive, is an angler worthy of a certain respect. The man who fishes the dry fly because he despises the worm or the wet fly may be accorded respect for the technique he employs, providing he is really dry-fly fishing and not cheating in a somewhat subtle way. Nevertheless, it is because of his kind that the word 'purist' has come to have a shade of meaning not entirely respectful!

In the ordinary sense of the word I admit to purism. The restriction is self-imposed and I seek to convert no one. I admire the wet-fly fisherman who may come along the bank and show me his creel containing more fish than I expect to catch. I have no feeling at all about the wormer. Presumably he gets what he seeks from the use of the worm. He doesn't really harm me so long as he doesn't take the last fish from the water; induce those that remain to become bottom feeders; or do anything to prevent a hatch of fly to which, I trust, my fish will ultimately rise!

If either the wormer or the wet-fly enthusiast think to comment on the sort of flies that adorn my hat—99 per cent of them are dry flies—I am ready to admit that I fish this way not because I think it a superior way of catching fish, or because I feel myself to be a superior sort of person, but because I love the technique above all else and nothing but the dry fly satisfies me. I can wait for my fish to rise. I can stand hours of waiting. I don't expect to fill my creel.

I often go empty away. But even on such occasions I sometimes go home satisfied that when the fish did rise and I cast to it, the fish turned and inspected the fly, took it if only half-heartedly, and beat me because I hadn't the wit to strike it, struck too soon or didn't leave the fly that second longer when it changed its mind and came again. If I cared what my fellow anglers thought of me as a catcher of trout I might contrive to conceal myself from them, or at least pretend that my creel was a great deal heavier than most of the time it is. One man's meat is another man's poison and a great deal depends on whether a man goes to the water to catch fish in a particular manner, or to satisfy himself in achievement of a certain standard.

How can one explain the precise business of seeing a fish rise, approaching the place, casting and hooking the fish after it has risen to the dry fly? It is a most individual and personal achievement. There is nothing quite like it except perhaps walking through a thicket to the known haunt of a woodcock, putting the bird up and shooting it. But even in shooting the bird there is a degree of doubt that it is precisely the bird that rose yesterday on the same feeding ground. I have known something close to the taking of a particular trout from a pool or behind a certain rock, in walking up a hare, or following a cock pheasant through a field of roots.

With great respect for the man who takes his stand to shoot driven birds, I think he misses as much as the fly fisherman who fishes blindly with a string of wet flies. And even the expert with the nymph is a degree removed from the individualistic experience of the man who presents the dry fly to the rising fish. This, of course, is my own personal feeling about the business. I am perhaps warped in that I find no other way satisfies me.

A close friend, who is an expert fisherman, regards me with some horror when we go together to a certain lake where fly-only is the rule although the angler may please himself as to wet or dry. I will stand and watch the surface of the lake while my colleague fishes steadily and industriously and perhaps lands one or two takeable fish. When I see fish rise, even a hundred yards away, I hasten to the spot and wait for it to show again before I try it with the dry fly. This, says my colleague, has the deliberation of a housewife exterminating the wasp. It isn't purism. It is predatory and beyond the limits of sportsmanship. He always smiles when he makes this accusation and I smile, too. I can't help myself because he can only make such a comment when I succeed in taking the fish I have stalked. When I do, I am transported, delighted, prepared to be called predatory or anything else a critic may choose to call me, for I have done the only thing I set myself as a standard in fly fishing.

I have pitted my wits against a rising fish, fooled it, battled it and taken it out of the water. Not a few times the fish has proved my master. And that's a good thing or there would be no joy in anything.

December 1963   *Ian Niall*

Trout vision and the fly fisher

The most important sense organ for shallow-water game fish such as the trout is sight, and it should be no surprise to us that trout do have excellent eyesight, perhaps far better than the average man's. Light diffusion and turbidity are limiting factors on under-water vision. Nevertheless, the trout possesses remarkable features of lens and retina, suggesting that its vision is acute over a wide range.

The vertebrate eye is basically the same organ whether in fish, in man or other vertebrates. However, there are a number of differences, such as the lack of eyelids and of sphincter and dilator muscles in fish. There are also many adaptive variations in the eyes of different species of fish.

The occular mechanism in the eye of higher fishes such as the trout appears to have developed towards heightened contrast and motion perception, in addition to the formation of sharp retinal images. Trout have colour vision—a faculty that appears to be limited to shallow-water species—and they also have the ability to see in dim light as well as in bright. Their retina is well provided with the two kinds of light-receptive cells: the cones, which act in bright light, and the rods, which take over in the dark.

Along with the other salmonids, trout have the peculiar ability of forming sharp retinal images of distant and nearby objects simultaneously. Their eyeball is slightly elliptical, with the long diameter parallel to the long axis of their body. The lens thus has two focal lengths, one that brings distant objects off to the side into focus on the centre of the retina, and the other focusing nearby objects in front on the rear of the retina. In the frontal field, the lens has a limited degree of accommodation.

The trout's visual contact with the aerial world passes through the so-called 'window' in the surface of the water. Most anglers know Dunne's or Harding's treatment of this phenomenon in their books or, if not, surely that of Dr Brown and Dr Frost. According to the laws of optics, the trout's field of vision from the water into the air is an inverted cone with its apex, of an angle of 97.6 degrees, at the trout's eye. Outside this angle—that is, 48.8 degrees on either side of the perpendicular from the eye to the surface—the underside of the surface is a mirror reflecting the bottom or objects in the water.

The nearer the fish to the surface, the smaller the window, since it is the base of a cone, and vice versa. However, through the effect of refraction, this conical field of vision opens out to the level of the surface in the air. The trout can thus see what is on the surface outside the window, but there is distortion on or near the surface. Nearby objects are indistinct, with fuzzy outlines, and distant objects appear smaller than they really are.

When the surface is disturbed by ripples or turbulence, the trout can no longer see out of its window and its visual contact with the outside is presumably broken off. That this is not entirely the case we all know from experience. A ripple helps the fisher to fool the keen eye of the trout, but it certainly does not blind it!

This summary of the characteristics of trout vision suggests a certain number of things for the fisher to keep in mind if he wants to be successful. For instance, since the trout cannot shield its eye from the sun other than by moving into the shade, it can be advantageous to have the sun at one's back (if no long shadows result) when approaching a trout in the sun from the side.

Some fishermen still hold that trout are colour-blind. Apart from the scientific evidence to the contrary, much practical experience and observation confirm that trout can see colours. Their extra-sharp contrast and motion perception can, under certain circumstances, make it seem they are indifferent to colour. This special ability to detect contrast and movement have obvious implications for the fisherman in his choice of clothing and in his comportment.

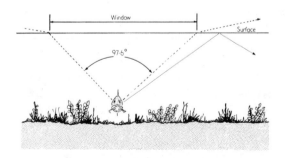

The trout's window in the surface. Reflection is total at an angle of incidence superior to 48.8 degrees for light rays travelling from a dense to a less dense medium. The reflection takes place from the surface separating the two media—in this case, the undersurface of the water

Sea-trout appear capable of distinguishing colours at night, and night fishing is generally considered best for these fish, as it is likewise for specimen browns in North America. We have another indication of the trout's ability to see in poor light in the rise to surface insects in water so dirtied by spates as to be opaque. No doubt they find worms or the like in such conditions by smell or 'distant touch' with the lateral line, but these two senses cannot account for their taking flies on the surface in water so thick it would be impossible for the human eye to see them, even in silhouette against the sky.

Can trout see colour and even delicate shades in silhouette against the sky? I am inclined to think they can, in daylight, although this point is debatable. What the trout finally sees as a colour is something we can probably never know, since it depends in part on subjective processes of interpretation and the like.

The big question is, how does our artificial on the surface appear to the trout? Besides what it sees through the window (including the distorted field along the surface), the trout also gets visual notice of an approaching non-immersed prey from the impression the latter makes on the surface; in the case of a dun, let us say, the imprint of its feet and body in the mirror. This image, corroborated by what the trout sees along the surface—probably only the wing tips—is likely to be enough indication that a familiar food item is coming, to decide the trout to take it on arrival in the window. This can only be hypothesis, but it seems to be borne out by the fact that dry flies in general look most lifelike from the side and least natural from underneath, as a trout would see them in its window.

Wary fish have learned to have another, harder look in the window and for these fish, special dressings, such as parachute or non-hackled patterns, may be the only answer, implying that hackle is the villain. This question has had a painstaking study in the United States by Swisher and Richards. On the other hand, the early images, such as the wing tips (or the hackle tips simulating them) seen along the surface, and the imprint in the mirror, vague and indistinct in all likelihood, look natural enough to decide the less sophisticated fish to nail the fly as soon as it enters the window.

Presumably, when the surface is agitated, the trout can see nothing in the window itself but vague silhouettes, and in the mirror area only distorted imprints of floating objects. Yet they seem able to see quite well through the surface turbulence—witness the selective rises to March Browns in fast water. Big fish in some waters prefer to lie under a screen of surface turbulence when they are on the rise.

Uniform ripples or waves, although they partially screen the trout's window to the aerial world, open others in the mirror area, since they bring sections of the surface momentarily within the 48.8 degrees angle beyond which light rays are reflected from the undersurface. There would be only a fleeting glimpse through each of these sections, but as there are a succession of them, the effect could be similar to what we experience when driving along a picket fence at the correct speed—the fence seems to disappear and we can see through it quite well.

The trout, then, can see very well, whether the surface is calm or not. If we have any doubts, all we have to do is watch them taking one particular kind of tiny insect—and only one—rapidly and repeatedly, out of a host of others.

June 1972   *George Beall*

The take of lake trout

A good deal of evidence is available on the rise-forms of river trout and how they take the surface fly and the underwater nymph, but much less has been written—I have, in fact, in some fairly extensive reading found nothing written at all—about the underwater take of lake trout. But there does seem to be a general assumption that lake trout take the fly savagely, more savagely than in rivers, and the term 'smash take' is heard frequently in lake fishing to describe the violent bang that one so often feels on the end of the line; in other words, that the take of a lake trout is a violent one.

The evidence I have suggests that it is not. I was particularly fortunate this season to be, as an observer, beside a small pond in Hampshire. It is quite small, not much more than 60ft across, and very shallow. Moreover it is fed by a chalk-stream so that the water is crystal clear, and there is little weed.

The takes of these trout—and they were large ones—were clearly visible and one could see the mouth open and close. In fact, the visibility was so good that on some occasions one could tell whether the trout was a brown or a rainbow. These are exceptional conditions but I do not see why experiences here should not have a general validity for bigger lakes like Chew and Blagdon and Grafham.

A young man was fishing this lake, a beginner who was being initiated into the arts and mysteries of the wet fly. He was using a cast with a single wet fly of standard pattern, or a nymph, in sizes from 14 down to 8. He cast in the direction of a single fish or groups of cruising fish and retrieved at varying speeds. Sometimes a slowly moving fish would quicken its speed slightly and follow the fly and take; at other times when the fly passed near a fish it would annex it, generally sideways, by a turn of the head and a slow movement of the body. There was no savagery in evidence.

The takes were gentle, almost idle and indolent, and there was no suggestion that the trout was putting out much energy even when it increased its speed to follow the fly—it was a gentle glide rather than a chase. The takes could be seen easily by the white line of the opening mouth—that is, they could be seen easily by me and by my companion, but not by the fisherman, mainly because of his inexperience, and in any case we were placing ourselves where reflections and water movements favoured the best visibility.

The fishing lasted four hours. During this time the rod was taken by a more experienced, though younger fisherman, for a brief period. His greater expertise made no difference to the results: during four hours I saw the fly taken by trout no fewer than fourteen times. There was no doubt about it. One could see the take and often, though not in all cases, the rejection. What was astonishing was the speed at which it was done. The take and the rejection appeared to be almost instantaneous. By the time we had seen the take and shouted 'strike', the ejection of the fly had taken place. The whole process of take and rejection was split-second—if one had to put a time to it one would say somewhere about a tenth of a second.

Out of the fourteen takes, only two trout were hooked and landed, one a good brown trout of about $1\frac{1}{4}$lb and the other a monster brown in first-rate condition of $4\frac{3}{4}$lb, which took twenty minutes to land. These fish were taken, in fact, because in both cases we shouted 'strike' slightly before the actual take occurred—that is, before we saw the white lines of the mouth.

The important thing to note about this whole affair, however, was not the speed of the take and rejection alone, but that in all the fourteen cases of a take, the anglers, whether experienced or inexperienced, felt nothing. In most cases, so far as I could judge, the line and cast were straight and the angler had the line in his hand and was retrieving at a reasonable speed—in at least two cases quite fast—yet, even so, the take and rejection process took place fourteen times without the angler feeling any pull or twitch or pressure at all. This seemed to me to be quite remarkable evidence of the ability of lake trout to take the fly many times without the angler knowing.

If these incidents have general validity and if the same processes of take and rejection are followed by lake trout in the opaque waters of larger lakes, certain conclusions follow that must to some extent affect our attitudes and techniques.

First of all, if lake trout take and reject so frequently compared with those hooked, by the middle and end of the season most of them must be assumed to be highly educated, and perhaps highly selective, in their choice of food.

Second, one can also assume that fast retrieves may stand a better chance of hooking a fish—not necessarily stripping but quick draws with the whole reach of the arm, followed perhaps by a slight pause.

Third, in order to increase the chance of seeing a take and therefore responding in time, one should try to fish as near the surface as possible. On this it is interesting that when I have been fishing dry fly for lake trout, the takes have been almost identical with the takes of river trout to the surface fly.

One final conclusion is perhaps possible. The 'smash take' is an illusion. What happens is that the trout has taken the fly and has felt the hook while the angler is still retrieving, and then, when the angler strikes, he adds additional and violent pressure and the trout responds equally violently. Similar pressure put on a river trout would inevitably produce the same result.

November 1969 *Conrad Voss Bark*

The deep nymph on big reservoirs

While I would not be foolish enough to suggest that any one method of fishing will succeed the whole of the time or that any one place will produce fish regardless of the conditions, I did, last year, find a marriage of two such considerations, which was successful on big reservoirs more often than it was not.

Success is, of course, a relative matter: but certainly this new (for me) approach succeeded in greatly increasing my average from these waters, compared with my results before. And it stemmed, curiously, from the sense of bewilderment felt on arriving at several square miles of water, with not a fish in sight.

When faced with a liquid Sahara, what on earth is the ordinary bank man to do? He is not a 'regular' in any real sense of the word; he does not know the water in any, much less all, of its moods; and, on the days he can get away, he has to take conditions as he finds them. He simply cannot get the experience that will permit a sensible evaluation of conditions and enable him to opt for 'such-and-such a technique, over there'. No doubt he will end up doing something of the sort, but it will be lucky dip, rather than diagnosis. And, when his choice is made, it will be sustained only for a while before the inevitable doubt sets in and the first of many moves and changes is made. In the end, and if he is lucky, he will go home with half a trout in his net, which seems to be the grisly average for bank anglers on big reservoirs.

All of this, certainly, is what happened in my own case, until I decided that attempting to 'read' the water was, for me, largely a futile exercise because I had no basis of knowledge from which to begin. I decided, instead, that my best approach would be to attempt to work out—and stick with—a formula that, if I could find it, would more often prove right than wrong.

If last year, therefore, there were fish to be seen rising within casting distance, then I cast gleefully to them: but that sort of luxury waited mostly for the evening rise, if it came at all. If no fish were rising, I opted to fish the deepest water I could reach, from a grassy bank. (At both Draycote and Grafham, which I visited several times, one may cast from the dams; but fishing from concrete is about as rewarding as changing nappies, and I avoid both if I am able.)

I chose deep water because: in cool weather, the fish were likely to find the deeper, warmer water, more hospitable; in hot weather, they were likely to find the deeper cooler water more hospitable; in shallow water they were continually harassed by wading anglers whereas, in deeper water, although they may be fished for hard, they could not often be driven physically from their feeding grounds (and so would be more likely to stay near the banks); I felt more confident if commonsense told me I could get within my own (rather limited) casting distance of fish; and so on. So deeper water it was. And because it also seemed more sensible, I persisted with patterns that represented or suggested natural, living foods.

It has been said many times before that stillwater trout obtain a good deal more of their food from the bottom than they do from the midwater or from the top. A decision to fish deep water, therefore, meant long leaders to get down to the fish. (I ruled out sinking lines from the start, because I am not confident that I can detect delicate takes with them.) And because fishing on the bottom using long leaders and floating lines meant that offers would be registered as movements of the floating line or the leader, this meant that I fished, whenever I could, into calm water where I could see both of them more easily.

Nine times out of ten, fishing into calm water meant fishing with the wind behind me, and this in turn conveyed further advantages: I could more easily cast the long leaders to which my decision to fish deep water had led me; and I would not be troubled with a faster, wind-blown upper layer of water, pushing my line (and in turn my fly) along at a wholly unnatural speed.

In practice, I found that the deepest water I could cover from the banks was 10–15ft, and I, therefore, needed leaders up to 25ft and even 30ft long. That struck me as a daunting length to cast, but again, in practice I found it comparatively easy, provided I did not worry too much if now and then it landed in a heap: and with the fish so far below, I had no need to worry at all. Because I was fishing at such a depth, I used a heavily leaded fly.

In order to cast the leader, I held the heavy fly in my left hand and then, with a couple of yards of line pulled through the top ring, I worked out more and more line with a series of mini-casts with the rod-top, while all the time retaining hold of the fly. When a sufficiently large loop was aerialised in front of me and I judged there was enough line out to flex the rod, I released the fly from my left hand, and went straight into a casting rhythm, in the normal way. It was all a great deal easier than it sounds and I rarely had any problems. Furthermore, if there was any kind of breeze at all, that, combined with the weight of the fly, turned the leader over cleanly.

I kept the end of my line—which is white, and comparatively easy to see—well greased, to make it float on top, and then simply fished as normal thereafter, watching the end of the line for signs of a take. (Incidentally, when is someone going to make a line that floats on, rather than in or under, the surface film? Such a product would be the biggest boon to fishing since the introduction of plastic lines themselves.)

It was an interesting characteristic of fishing this method that 'smash' takes were not at all uncommon. In normal nymph fishing, provided the nymph is being moved slowly, a smash take has, in my experience, been a rare occurrence: in fishing the deep nymph, one take in three or four (that I could see) would be made with great violence, often pulling the entire length of line deep down into the water, as though the fish has bolted with the fly. (I suppose that this, indeed, is a possibility. My hooks were always lightly dressed and needle sharp, and I suppose the fish might have panicked on feeling the point—in which case it would not really be a violent take I would be seeing, but the reaction of a startled trout making off with a hook already pricking it, some moments after the real take had occurred.)

Another interesting characteristic of the deep nymph was that it accounted for almost as many brown trout as for rainbows; and, odd though it may seem, most of the smash takes, or bolting takes, came from these. The flies I used varied, but generally I used large (sizes 6, 8 and 10) caddis or beetle-like patterns tied especially for fishing the bottom. Other anglers I saw fishing the deep nymph at Grafham were equally successful using leaded Muddler Minnows or Jersey Herds, so I cannot think that pattern is of critical importance. Depth is, however and likewise movement. The fly needed to be right on the bottom and moved with infinite patience and slowness.

My visits to Draycote, Grafham and other big reservoirs where I fished this method produced returns of 1-4-2-2-8-0-2-0-4. All these fish were taken from the bank, and, although the returns will not be startling to many anglers, they would be (and were!) a welcome change to someone formerly averaging 0.5 or a little more, per outing. What is more, I am confident that had I been able to get in more practice, I would have had more fish still. The trick is to see the offers, and hit them. And with a 30ft leader, that can be more easily said than done.

February 1974 *Brian Clarke*

Keep on the move

On many of my early visits to Midlands reservoirs, when I did not know a great deal about reservoir fishing, I used to follow the apparently general custom of finding myself a likely looking spot and of staying in that area all day. Admittedly, in the early days of Grafham, in particular, one could be forced to do this because the easy upwind shores tended to be rather crowded and the angler who forsook his chosen claim for more than a moment or two would be bound, on his return, to find it filled by some other enthusiast.

However, with increasing experience and confidence, I found myself regularly questioning, or criticising, what to many may seem to be the properly established and normal practices. As a result, one of the first questions I asked myself was: 'Why do so many bank anglers apparently accept that they must stay in the same spot, if not all day, then at least for several hours?'

The answer seemed to be that in general one chose a special place perhaps by habit, perhaps because it looked good, but above all because one was confident of being able to catch something there—and in my opinion confidence is an essential ingredient of success.

On a reservoir such as Grafham, where there are miles of shoreline, it may initially pay to fish regularly along several shortish lengths of bank in order to get to know the layout of bottom, weedbeds, snags and so on. Although the fish may not be showing or apparently moving when the angler arrives, the chances are that at some time during the day there will be some activity in his vicinity and that he will have some sport.

For example, all Grafham anglers must have experienced those late summer evening rises when the fish gradually move in from deep water until they are within range of the rows of hopeful bank fishermen. However, to remain firmly rooted to one spot, or even a small area, for any length of time will inevitably mean in the long run a considerable reduction in success, because during the day, and often in the evening also, fish may well be moving along on only a short stretch of bank and nowhere else at all.

Everyone must have experienced those desperately frustrating times when the next-door fisherman, using the same flies, fishing at the same distance and in the same manner as yourself, has managed to catch a limit while you have had a blank. Sometimes this happens because he is doing something slightly differently, but this is by no means always the case.

For example, the contours of the bottom, or the position of the weedbeds, may be funnelling fish in towards him while anglers on

either side are fishing empty water. If you are in any doubt about the reasons for your lack of success, the only thing to do is move.

Again it is a well-known fact that rainbows tend to shoal and if one can find the fish, a good bag is assured. I well remember bank anglers in the early days of Grafham checking the return cards from the previous day with the bailiffs in order to find out where most of the fish had been caught. Obviously, unless he is lucky, a fisherman will not find these fish by going to and remaining in just one spot.

All of us who regularly fish a particular water must have our own special 'hot-spots'. For example, two experienced Grafham fishermen tell me that they reckon that there are only about eight such places around Grafham's shores, and I can think of only six on what was, until recently, my own local water, Siblyback. On arriving on the bank the angler tends to head directly to one of these favourite places, but if the fish are not moving or are proving difficult the experienced fisherman will move on.

Time and time again it has been this willingness to move that has resulted in my having some success when otherwise I may well have had a blank, and yet I still see fishermen wasting time and energy by standing in exactly the same position all day. Apart from anything else, how soul-destroying and dull it must be, and how can such an angler ever learn his water well or find his own 'hot-spots'?

On mentioning my thoughts on this subject to another keen angler while on the water during last season, I was accused of being patronising. Nothing could be further from my mind. All I want to do is to help the less experienced angler to improve his catch. Anyway, facts are facts and, as I have already said, a large number of fishermen just do not bother to move, but waste time and money flogging away at totally unproductive water.

Somehow I think that it is this image of stillwater fishermen, standing firmly in one spot, lashing an apparently featureless patch of water into foam, which for a long time caused them to be looked upon with such scorn by their friends, the river fishermen. It is an image that is totally false, but it will be so only if we really do make the effort to get the most out of our water by learning to know it well. This means by expending a little energy on going to look for the fish, rather than expecting them to come to us.

February 1972 *Pat Gage*

But I call him 'Sir'

My fellow anglers called him Sam, but to me the diminutive ill-fitted his stately person. Meaty he certainly was, but with equal certainty he was not matey. Though he lived in the age of the common man, he was not of it. By temperament he was of the Age of Elegance. Thus I knew him as Samuel.

He lay within a cave of alder shoots, into which the current was diverted by a weed-bed. It was an extremely well-appointed residence. The green ribbing of the alders filtered sunlight pleasantly, yet provided shade. Wavering watery breezes fanned the leaves and ripples played about the woodwork. Life within was unhurried, tranquil and free from all rude intrusions through flank and rear of the cave. The current was just enough to carry food at a gentle pace into Samuel's sanctuary. He never had to go outside that rustic arbour. All he had to do was to cruise up to the opening or drop back to the rear, which he did in accordance with the stages of his meal.

For the hors-d'oeuvre he would lie 2ft below the opening, giving himself sufficient time to ponder the tit-bits as they came into view. For the main course he would drop back to the centre, where he would enjoy himself with all the delicate appreciation of the true gourmet; no vulgar lipsmacking, no aggressive gulping, but a gentlemanly savouring of choice fare. When nearly replete, he would retreat to the end of his cave, there to toy with the biscuits and cheese. Then he would sink to the cool depths, slowly, majestically. Had he belched, it would not have been the belch of gluttony, but of thanks.

As befitted the occupant of such a luxurious abode, waited on hand and foot, knowing nothing of how the poor live, Samuel waxed fat and perhaps a trifle lazy, but he was a trout who had knocked about the world in his youth, and in moments recollected in tranquillity a knowing gleam would light his eye and you would realise that here was no flabby decadent, but one who was wise in the ways of things that looked like flies but hid sharp little points. He stored this knowledge within his brain and now it brought him much amusement as I discovered when I set about his downfall.

Assault in any aggressive sense was unthinkable. Such tactics would have been treated with the patrician contempt they deserved; to have slapped any old mess in front of Samuel would have been like slapping down egg and chips in front of a noble lord at four o'clock in the afternoon.

So for a time I did nothing but lie prone amid the bankside grass, with binoculars trained on every movement of my quarry during his dinner, and that was how I came to acquaint myself with his gradual withdrawal from front to rear of his cave as the meal progressed, and with that recollective orb.

It soon became evident that his laziness was more apparent than real, and physical only. Mentally, he was as alert as anyone half his age and refusals were not due to inertia, but reflected his epicurean tastes. To catch him on the verge of napping was just not on. By the time slumber began to stroke his eyeballs he had back-pedalled to the end of his lair, and to offer him anything there would have been as futile as blowing thistle-down through a blackberry bush. Likewise, his position for the main course was secure from knavish tricks.

The only stage where Samuel was in the least vulnerable was the hors d'oeuvre, since his place for this allowed the possibility of floating something down. But it was a slim chance. Hooking from upstream is ticklish; if Samuel ignored my offering its retrieve would set his nerves on edge. Would it be better in this event to flip it back quickly, or to pull it out stealthily? In the former case I stood some chance of snagging up in his arbour; in the latter, he would surely spot that odd-looking object drawing away from him.

I had to get upstream, pitch just below the weed bed into that nonchalant but cornucopian little current, and pray to Ate, the divine goddess of mischief. Samuel always began with nymphs. To float a nymph down on a line tight enough to allow for immediate contact at the crucial moment, but never to arrest its progress even for a split-second as it sails into the trout's vision, demands a co-ordination of reflexes denied to most ordinary mortals, but now and again I catch a grayling or two on the downstream cast, so surely if I could hook that lunging creature, there should be a hope of hooking the placid Samuel?

One thing was certain: I would need a good ten minutes between any failures, and time was vital, for he seldom spent more than twenty minutes nymphing, and usually withdrew to his middle station as soon as the duns came down. Would my nymph look more edible dropped into the swirl immediately below the weed or dropped a foot lower into the glide?

It seemed to me a question of enormous weight, though on later reflection I doubted whether Samuel cared two hoots where it was dropped. Anyway, on the principle of first things first, I pitched it, from behind a clump of willow herb, into the swirl, with cast greased almost to the tip, for I knew that Samuel preferred his nymphs just below the surface.

It was a nice little Partridge and Orange, thinly hackled. It went into Samuel's cave with the loveliest precision, and he, more trusting than I had dared believe possible, sucked it in. But his long experience came to his aid, even after three years of sybaritic living, and as I struck I knew that I had not even lightly connected, for I struck nothing but void.

Thus began a season's effort that took me through every nymph pattern that man's ingenuity had devised. Never more than two casts an evening never less than ten minutes between each. But Samuel had learned his lesson. He did not take again and as time went by I could almost hear him snigger, 'Here comes that old fool again.' On other occasions I seemed to see his arbour gently vibrating and put it down to his shaking sides.

But I must not place him in the past tense, for he is still there, jovial, dignified, fat and happy. Sometimes I think he winks a sardonic eye as I pass. But I do not wink back, for Samuel would not like familiarity from a social inferior. I bow, bid him good evening and pass on. And I always call him Sir.

March 1971   *D Macer Wright*

Rise-forms of trout

For successful fly fishing for trout, it seems fundamental to know three things: exactly where your fish is; whether it is feeding; and if so, on what it is feeding. In every circumstance this may not be absolutely necessary nor infallible; few statements on fish and fishing are, yet it is a fairly safe assumption.

I know the 'chuck and chance it' method of fishing two or more flies is claimed as productive as any on certain waters, but for the dry-fly man on the chalk-stream at least, a more precise knowledge is required before he puts many trout into the bag.

The fact is, a feeding trout is one most likely to repeat the performance and to stick to its original choice, and for the angler with the dry fly this makes the 'rise' important. Obviously it tells him where his fish is and that it is on the feed; also, if read aright, the manner of it will lead him a long way towards selecting the right tying from his box.

A 'rise' to the fisherman, can be described as a surface disturbance caused by a feeding fish. But it does not necessarily follow that every rise means a feed has been made at the water's surface. According to its character, besides being to a winged fly on the surface, a rise can also denote a near-surface feed or one considerably deeper, even off a river's bed. It depends on the nature of the disturbance and what part or parts of a fish caused it.

When an angler sees a rise he must decide whether it was from the head, the back or even the tail of a fish; because a rise may not be a rise at all in the factual sense. It can be caused by a fish going down—a dive and not a rise. So we come to the first significance of rise-form and what it has to tell us. But first we must know something of how a trout takes certain items of its diet.

Every angler knows the fondness a trout has for freshwater shrimp. If a fish is seeking these in a shallow run and is of any length, as it picks them off the bottom so will the surface of the run be broken by the elevated tail. In the same way a fish feeding upon a raised weed-bed, whether to shrimp or anything else, will often air its tail.

As a rule this is not difficult to spot, as the tail waving can sometimes be considerable. In addition, after each capture such a trout can be seen to drift backwards a little with the stream, while it appears to chew over what it has taken. In angling nomenclature 'it

Rise-form to olive dun

will tail', and a tailing trout has no need of any surface fly, however tastefully tied or offered.

Another tail-made disturbance in danger of being mistaken for a proper rise is the one that occurs near any river posts, by camp-sheathing, or the like. This may indicate a fish diving for those egg-laying spinners that stick their eggs to such underwater sites. An ordinary fly fished dry will have little attraction here.

But a trout taking near-surface nymphs on their way to hatching is another matter. If the take is delayed until the nymph is in the act of passing by a fish, or has actually passed, an extra swirl may be added to the normal 'humping' of the nymphing fish. This can be made by the back fin or the tail, or both, as the trout suddenly turns to regain its original lie, and can be easily mistaken for a true rise.

However, any trout after nymphs should be watched carefully, even on dry-fly-only water. Such a fish will often turn its attention to a winged fly or one in the process of kicking free of its shuck on the surface, especially if some hitch has occurred in the hatching. This is more probable when the swirl is preceded by a V-formed disturbance across stream, indicating that the fish has swung considerably to one side in order to secure the insect.

A fish that does this usually proves more interested in an offering at the surface than one that stays put. For this reason the cast of some rough-hackle tying, according to the duns hatching, should also be to one side of where the fish lies. And given a little drag, this will prove more attractive than one floated quietly directly overhead.

All this is a little obvious, but more subtle perhaps, when we come to the rises to winged flies, because every fly, or type of fly, produces its own particular rise-form. Of course, merely recognising the difference is not enough, nor does the knowledge work like magic. It has to be used and related to all the circumstances of the rise: season, time of day, place and condition of water, as well as the flies suspected to be on the water.

Primarily rise-form in the true rises can be roughly divided between those to insects likely to escape and those that are unlikely to do so. In fact, as would seem natural, the degree of disturbance is an index to the trout's anxiety. Either this may show itself in the grabbing tactics caused by an intense liking for a particular fly, as in the case of the typical slashing rise to the mayfly, or it may be the result of hurry.

The rise to most escaping insects is not only violent, but the form is distinct; it has a direction; it is a rise taken on the run as it were. Large evening sedges fluttering along the surface is one cause of the predatory rise; another is a wind-blown crane fly. Under trees struggling moths can be suspected, or if near overhanging grassy banks grasshoppers are often responsible for smashing takes.

Similarly the smaller sedges, caperers, a fluttering alder fly, will produce this type of rise, though correspondingly less violent than those to larger, faster insects. A good hatch of iron blue duns will

Kidney rise

often stimulate an unusual eagerness in trout, making the rise to these flies quite characteristic.

On big rivers such as the Usk, and when carrying a good wave, the keenness with which trout will respond to an iron blue hatch is recognised by the manner in which the feeding trout will thread waves like so many silver needles going through a puckered cloth.

To the blue-winged olive on a chalk-stream the rise is no less characteristic, and is surprisingly constant in form. No violence here, but the rise always leaves a curious double whirl on the surface, of two intersecting rings. Often called the 'kidney rise', it is a sure sign that blue-winged olives are being taken.

A single simple ring or series of rings widening from a common centre, with a bubble, or perhaps two or three left in the middle, usually means that the attraction is a large upright winged fly such as the big olives, or a large spinner that sits well up on the water.

This rise-form is best seen in the smoother waters of bays and is often accompanied by an audible sucking noise. It seems to be the largeness of the wings which occasions the suck because I have noticed, mayflies apart, the larger the fly the louder the sucking. The bubbles are no doubt expended air drawn in with the fly.

But this particular sucking must not be confused with the 'sip'. Though equally audible, this rise leaves behind no bubble and is a much quieter affair altogether, usually causing little more than the merest dimple at the surface. This is how trout will take the pupae of chironomids that hang suspended in the surface film of many of our reservoirs. But in the rivers it can mean a rise to reed smuts and their like, or to the smaller spent spinners. If on an evening following a shower after much dancing of spinners under trees there are such dimples together with the sipping in the quieter reaches of the stream, the angler may be sure that a good fall of spinners is the reason.

This, in a general way, is what rise-form means to the angler. It needs a quick eye, which most anglers have, and the ability to read the writing on the water. To do this correctly helps him with his fly-box and his fishing.

May 1957   *G A Grattan*

Bad connections

During a lifetime of fishing I must have cast my flies back and forth many thousands of miles, and I suppose it was inevitable that at times I should have hooked some unusual objects.

Once when I was fishing alongside the gable end of the Tap Cottage on the Bull Hotel water on the Colne at Fairford, I was trying to cover a trout rising right under the far bank and did not realise that my back cast was going over the main road—until I felt a snag.

Looking round, I found that I had hooked a woman on a bicycle. Had I hooked her person it would not have turned out too badly, but no, I had hooked her shopping basket, which was tied to her back carrier. Oblivious to my dilemma, she peddled on towards Cirencester.

I splashed my way out of the river and gave chase, but she looked round, saw a wild-looking young man running after her, and increased speed—with the inevitable result that my line was stripped right out until the leader broke at the fly, leaving me to wind back line and backing along the dusty road.

I have hooked many swallows, swifts and martins, but one day on the Derbyshire Derwent I was back-casting a long line in a strong wind when it whipped across my face and I found a Greenwell's Glory firmly embedded in the tip of my nose.

Now the tip of the human nose consists of a little lump of gristle without blood or nerves which is quite capable of resisting all attempts to remove a hook. I wound up, cut off the fly, tied on another and carried on fishing. But although the hook was only a size 12, it looked like a bird and I found myself becoming cross-eyed.

I soon gave up and returned to the hotel, where the barmaid produced a pair of pliers. We tried to cut through the wire, but without success. There was no doctor in the village, so I was directed to the village nurse, who unfortunately lived in some remote back street necessitating several enquiries from locals, all of whom showed great surprise at my unusual appearance. It became so embarrassing that I had to produce my handkerchief and pretend that I was wiping my nose while making enquiries.

Eventually I ran the old girl to ground. She was most sympathetic, but quite useless, producing an enormous pair of cutting-out scissors with which she gripped the fly at the point of entry while I tried to break it off by wriggling the eye sideways. Soon the scissors slipped ... that little bit of nose is missing to this day.

For five consecutive years before the last war I went to Lough Derg on the Shannon for the mayfly dapping. After the first year I became rather frustrated at the limited range of the dap and decided in future to use my dry fly, concentrating on an all-hackle pattern that was to prove most effective.

Now Lough Derg has many islands, and we used to land and brew up tea. On one particular occasion we had joined up with two other boats of dappers, but my uncle had seen a good trout rising regularly about 50yd out and had gone off in the boat by himself.

Then Florrie and Maureen arrived in another boat to join the tea party, and Florrie announced her intention to paddle out and join my uncle. It was a warm sunny day and she tucked her dress into her knickers and set forth.

The trouble started as soon as she pressed down on the gunwale. The boat tipped sideways, her feet floated up under the keel and all that was visible from the bank was the floral design on her pants bobbing up and down like a yo-yo.

The temptation was too great. I waded in and lengthened my line until I achieved a cast that would have won a first prize in any dry-fly accuracy competition. My spent gnat landed right on target. I struck and the damage was done. Fortunately, the hook was in the material and not actually in Florrie, but my uncle had to pull her on board, put on his specs, up-end her and cut out the hook.

My uncle, alas, has now gone to ground for good, and his ashes are scattered at a point where three counties meet and where the foxes rear their cubs. But before he departed I did manage to hook him firmly in the back of his neck. The resulting language put down all the fish in the area, and although he was my mother's brother, he even cast doubt on my parentage.

April 1976   *Stanley Woodrow*

Evenings on the lakes

I have always believed that every marrow scoop should be sold together with a shotgun. Useful though the scoop is, it is ironic that it can show only what a captured fish has eaten, for when one most desperately wants this information, fish seem impossible to come by. However, it's a fair bet that those intense evening rises in late June, through July and August, are activated by small midge (chironomid) pupae, or buzzers as anglers usually call them.

These pupae may be much smaller than most anglers realise. There seems to be a school of thought, mistaken in my opinion, that, on big waters particularly, big fish must be offered a big fly. One can't be dogmatic about these things—and, regrettably, I don't catch big fish as often as I would like (do any of us?)—but 'big' is a relative term anyway and if one reads for 'big', 'reasonably big' and considers three- to four-pounders, then I can see from my records that a large percentage of these fish are caught on a small fly once July arrives. One need only consider the water where a hook size restriction is imposed to see that fish that are big by any standards are caught on comparatively small hooks.

The late spring buzzer rises didn't materialise to any degree last season because of the poor weather. The cream of that season's buzzer fishing started for me in mid-June, by which time size 8 and 10 imitations were too big; 12s were accepted, but as the year progressed 14s and 16s were necessary.

I enjoyed some marvellous evening fishing on Chew Lake in June and July last season. The daytime was often unproductive under the cloudless skies, but by the time the yachting was over for the day some great buzzer rises occurred off the boat stations. In spite of this, many boats went in clean. It wasn't difficult to see why. But it must be frustrating to wait all day for the rise and then to miss out on it when it comes. It happens to all of us at times, but a little thought and expertise would save many a blank.

I don't get much of a kick out of lure fishing at the best of times, but to fish a lure in the middle of a frenzied buzzer rise seems ludicrous to me. The Butcher, Peter Ross and Zulu are all lures to my way of thinking, however small the hook. I much prefer to get my fish on an imitation of a known food item (granted this may include fish fry at times), and these are the fish I feel I have deserved. I can appreciate that some do not care at all as long as they get results. That's fair enough, but some anglers are so narrow-minded and their technique so stereotyped that their overall catch is significantly affected.

So many times during an evening rise I have seen a single lure or cast of traditional lake flies put out and retrieved in a mechanical, repetitive fashion. This may be all right in a big wave when there is no specific rise on, but most evening rises are on stillwater with little or no ripple. During these frenzied rises, when pupae are plentiful, it takes a lot of luck to knock a fish off balance and to make it take something quite different. You'll get one now and again, but most of those hooked come unstuck. It is far better to offer a reasonable imitation and induce a confident take for a decent hookhold. Perhaps so many anglers dislike calm water because they fail to adapt their technique and tackle accordingly.

To be blind to the complexities of trout feeding habits denies one not only a great deal of interest and pleasure, but opportunity, too. So often I have seen big food items ignored and much smaller ones taken with avidity, purely because they have been present in far greater numbers. On several occasions last season the mayfly suddenly lost its appeal because of a bigger hatch of small lake olives. Those who didn't recognise the situation missed out for a while until the mayfly came back into favour. Likewise, I have often seen liberal quantities of alders refused because of a big fall of greenfly.

Many more such instances come to mind, and one could postulate that a size 8 Mallard and Claret is ignored in a buzzer hatch not because of its artificiality, but because it is obviously outnumbered by the pupae. One would think that the bigger food item would be taken with relish, but trout don't appear to have small-boy minds at these times. Quantity, not quality, seems to be their criterion.

The characteristic head-and-tail rise of the early season buzzer activity gives way to quite a different performance once the pupae become smaller and more numerous. With so much food in the surface film, the feeding pattern is different and fishing technique must be altered accordingly. In early days a fish will often take a pupa on the drop or just as it starts to rise again as the line is given tension. Furthermore, they will often deviate from the feeding line if the cast has not been accurate. In summer this approach doesn't seem to be effective. With the surface literally thick with food, fish don't have to cruise a few feet down in order to scan a big area; they swim along with their noses out and often look deceptively small.

Having decided on the correct size of pupa imitation, the difficult thing is to present it at the right time and place. Without the influence of wind or drift, fish don't move in a predetermined direction, and to anticipate the feeding line requires a certain measure of luck. At Chew I found it futile to put the fly down on their noses, however delicately, as one does in the early season. It is difficult to resist this temptation, but I have found that one must put down at least 3yd in front, and that's where the difficulty arises. With fish zig-zagging all over the place, they are just as likely to go off on quite a different line.

When a fish does take an obliging course, I give the line a little tension, which serves to lift the artificial back into the surface film again, when the fish is about 3ft away. Additional working of the fly is seldom effective.

For this type of fishing I like to use a double-tapered size 6 line with at least 12ft of nylon leader, consisting of a length of 20lb b.s. nail-knotted directly to the end of the line, and finished off with a 3yd knotless tapered 4x cast.

Last season a friend gave me a pupa pattern that, when modified slighty for convenience of tying materials, exploded tbe belief put forward by the great Cyril Inwood that smooth-bodied midge pupa patterns are not at all effective. I had always believed it and would have never learned otherwise had I not tried my friend's pattern in desperation one night. Response was immediate.

The fly, as I now tie it, is put on to a wide-gape hook as follows, in order of tying in:

Tail Short tuft of white fluorescent floss tied in right round the bend of the hook

Body Fluorescent DRF wool teased out thinly and spun on to the silk, first two turns red, remainder phosphor yellow

Over-body Clear PVC strip about $\frac{1}{16}$ in wide

Rib Copper wire coloured bright green (rod-whipping nylon would suffice)

Breathing tubes Short tuft of white fluorescent wool over eye of hook

Thorax Olive goose herl, not too bulky.

This pattern was used to considerable effect from mid-June to July in sizes 12 and 14, catching good fish in difficult conditions. By mid-

July the magic appeared to wear off a little, and it was then that I tied up an orange version, substituting fire-orange DRF for the yellow, a rib of red wire and a thorax of dark brown turkey tail fibres. This one really did the trick at Chew in sizes 14 and 16.

Quite frankly I am intoxicated by the excitement of buzzer fishing, particularly in calm water. Though I don't keep records to prove it, I take most of my fish in calm water on whatever fly. Boat companions who don't know me better often look in disbelief when I enthuse over the prospects of a flat calm. A breeze will often terminate a buzzer rise and silverhorns will disappear instantly the wind rises. But of course, there are flat calms and flat calms. On one occasion in August, Chew Lake had a surface-temperature of over 70°F—and that isn't going to bring anyone much joy. But when fish are showing it should be possible to latch on to a few of them.

February 1973   *Derek Bradbury*

Guest on the water

Today I have a guest coming to fish our water. He is a very important person to me, and it is essential that he has a good day's sport. He is among those fortunate people who wallow in this world's goods. His shining, immaculate vehicle will arrive soundlessly outside my front door at eleven o'clock precisely. Neighbours will poke their heads out of their windows as I go out nonchalantly to meet him. I shall invite him in for a coffee or a glass of sherry, but he will not come then. So I shall transport my gear ostentatiously out to his car, hoping as many folk as possible see me doing so.

My guest is the owner of broad policies of land. The fat sheep and cattle of his tenants graze there contentedly. He has large and well-stocked coverts. In the spring the cock pheasants strut about beating their wings and challenging the rest of the world. Their wives, less obtrusive, watch them proudly. Throughout the summer their progeny lead a sheltered life, nurtured and keepered. In the winter they take to the coverts and hedgerows. Then, if my guest remembers my existence and thinks favourably of me, I get a day's shooting.

My guest has a cottage in Scotland and a mile of river with it. It is not a famous river, but more often than not salmon are in the pools. If salmon are not there, well, the sea-trout always are. Besides these there are brown trout in plenty. It is beautifully situated in the foothills of the mountains and the sea is only a mile or so away. It is just the place for a family holiday, in fact. Perhaps if I drop a hint or two during the day—not blatantly, of course—who knows?

I have done everything possible to make the day a success. Yesterday I marked down several good fish that seemed to be steady risers. There was a fine hatch of mayfly and fish were coming for them as though they had not fed for months. There was every chance we would have the water to ourselves on a mid-week afternoon. I had not offended any of the piscatorial gods by promising anyone I would catch a trout for them. The weather was fine and the wind gentle, although it had shifted a point or two to the north. In fact, everything pointed to the fact that I could not have chosen a better day to take my guest fishing.

At eleven o'clock precisely, as I had predicted, his sleek monster glided to a stop outside my door. There are rod racks on each side of the car, and badges supporting numerous worthy causes below the radiator. The door opens soundlessly as I walk forward to it.

'So glad you could make it,' I say. 'Do come in for a coffee or a gin.'

'I had a coffee just before I left and I never imbibe gin before twelve o'clock,' came the reply.

'Come in when we get back, then . . . I'll get my gear.'

So my rod bag and waders are deposited in the cavernous boot, and we are away.

I tell him of my reconnaissance and the fish I saw rising yesterday. He tells me of his last trip to Scotland, where he landed eleven salmon and countless sea-trout during the week he spent at his retreat. 'It's let to an American until the late autumn . . . awfully nice chap . . . got his own plane and promised to fly me over for a go at steelhead, and possibly a moose.'

One of my dreams fades. There are still the pheasants, though.

We reach the river bridge. The sun shines on the yellow wings of mayfly duns fluttering aimlessly above the parapet. I look over the bridge and the water is the colour of strong cocoa. It is quite hopeless to fish a fly over it, for no fish would ever see anything on the surface. I cannot understand it, for it was as clear as chalk-stream water yesterday, and there has been no rain.

Then I hear a bellow upstream and realise our landlord has moved his awesome Friesian bull, with attendant cows, into the next field upstream. With the sun hot above, most of the cattle are in the water under the trees, stirring up the mud and defecating as they swish their black tails at the flies on their flanks. The stretch below them will be useless until the early evening, when they should come out of the water and start to graze.

Meanwhile, my friend is putting up his rod. I explain what has happened and say we will move on upstream and return in the evening. We have plenty of good water to choose from and I am still full of confidence.

I guide him through narrow lanes where the hedges scrape the sides of his monster to our next bridge upstream. There is no car parked there so we must be first on the water. We both put up our rods and put our waders on and lumber over the stile on to the river bank. The river follows a convoluted pattern of bends and is heavily bushed in many places. I send my guest on ahead and sit on the bank while he goes.

Fly is hatching, plenty of it. Mayflies (which I always recognise), medium-sized yellow flies (which I knowingly term olives), and little black flies (which I call black gnats). My more expert friends call them ephemera or *Bibio* something or other, a territory into which I dare not venture unless I am sure that my companion knows less than I know. As I sit there, watching flies and idly musing, it suddenly strikes me with the force of a sledge-hammer that no trout are rising at all, despite the delicacies floating over their noses.

Trout are always contrary brutes. Even so, some should be showing. It is too early in the day for them to be gorged. So what can be the reason for their non-appearance? It is soon made all too plain. I hear voices approaching and two revolting fellow-members of the club come downstream, their bags hanging heavy on their shoulders. I know them well. They are a pair of schoolmasters. Such folk are always having free periods or some other reason for time off and get on the water at most unpredictable times.

'Wonderful morning,' one says.

'Great hatch of fly. We both got a limit,' smirks the other.

'Went over this pretty thoroughly. Got a fish of $1\frac{1}{4}$lb just on that bend.'

'They've gone off now. It was great while it lasted.'

And so they babble on with similar inanities, having crudely flogged the water to death and put down every rising fish.

'By the way,' one says, 'there was a stranger upstream. Said somebody had brought him along as a guest; promised him a full bag of trout.'

'He'll have to work jolly hard here,' says the other idiot.

They go on downstream. The swine had driven their car down a farm track and walked across the field to the river. That was why I never realised that anyone was above us. I must get to my guest quickly and move him on to the next bridge.

He has gone a long way and when I reach him the sweat is streaming copiously from my brow. I explain what has happened and suggest that we move upstream again. He has not seen a fish rise, either. But he has met the two schoolmasters and says what nice chaps they are. One knows the district near his beat in Scotland, and the other has promised to'tie some salmon flies for him. I know who will be going to Scotland . . .

We toil downstream to the bridge and get in the car. The leather seats are so hot that they nearly remove the skin from our posteriors. I am baked, parched and dehydrated. It is mid-day and the cool low-ceilinged bar of the local pub calls almost irresistibly. But when I suggest it, a large Thermos of tea is proffered in lieu. So we drink hot tea and eat oily buttered sandwiches inside the hot-house atmosphere of the car. I listen to stirring tales of Stock Exchange coups, mighty salmon caught and astronomic totals of driven pheasants.

At last the car starts up again and a cool breeze blows on me. We thread our way through more lanes and get on to a beat yet further upstream. I have not been there since last season and I have to admit it looks a bit overgrown. However, there are open places, as I explain. We walk upstream and come to such a pool. As we approach there is a furious rise to a struggling mayfly. The fish is near to the top of the pool and a branch of an alder sweeps low over the water just in front.

'Have a go at him,' I say hopefully. 'You can get in there with a roll cast.'

The first cast is short, but on the second the fly curls lovingly around a twig. Jerking will not dislodge it, so my friend pulls hard and the branch comes towards him and flies back, violently depositing, when the nylon breaks, a heap of twigs and dead leaves over the fish which had risen.

Meanwhile the fly falls on to the surface and is drifting unattached across the pool when another fish, in quite open water, rises, engulfs it, then spits it out. I urge my friend to hasten with another fly.

This fish is a sitter and he is sure to get it. But the contrary brute has had enough of artificials and lies smugly on the bottom.

We go on up the river. I am getting quite desperate. There is another break in the serried alders and moved by some impulse I cast a fly a few yards upstream. A trout rises the instant the fly touches the water, and a minute later I have the embarrassment of landing a fish of more than 1lb, despite all my efforts to shake it off. I can hear my guest's teeth grinding on his pipe.

'You've got them well trained up here,' he says ironically.

In the next pool he lands a fish, but it is only about half the size of mine and he puts it back in disgust. Then a better fish comes unstuck as he is about to net it. And so the dreadful day goes on. We end up with three fish between us, of which I have been unlucky enough to catch two. He will not come in for a drink when we get home and is engaged elsewhere on all the days I suggest he should come again. I fear I shall never catch one of his salmon or shoot one of his pheasants. Damnation on all fish, but especially trout!

September 1976   *Frank Morris*

Times when it pays not to drift

Having just completed a study of all I can find in the way of books and articles about loch-fishing, from Hamish Stuart onwards, I am struck by the fact that there is universal acceptance of the value of fishing from a drifting boat and of the idea that feeding trout are not found in or over very deep water.

My experience of fishing the waters in Scotland and Ireland that seem to have formed the basis for these ideas is relatively small, but I have done enough fishing on large water-supply reservoirs in the Midlands, the south of England and in the West Country to know that, more often than not, the angler who anchors his boat on these waters will catch more trout than the drifter; and that often, trout are to be caught where the water is deepest, sometimes near the surface, sometimes at depths of 40ft or more.

There are, of course, great differences between water-supply reservoirs on the one hand, and the various sorts of loch and lough on the other. Among these differences, we may include the nature of the bottom and the numbers of anglers on the banks.

A water-supply reservoir has a bottom that is, as a rule, made of what was once fertile agricultural land. Even at a depth where there may be a low level of dissolved oxygen in the water in summer, there are many insects that can thrive in their larval form. Consequently we often find hatches of some of the chironomid species occurring over water as deep as 60–70ft. Needless to say, trout feed on these insects and provide the fly fisher with excellent opportunities, which he will certainly miss if he has been led to believe that trout are found only where the water is 12ft deep or less.

On popular reservoirs, the effect of large numbers of wading bank anglers is two-fold. First, it is most discourteous on the part of boat anglers to approach nearer to a wading bank angler than 100yd; second, wading by numbers of anglers tends to deny access by the trout to the shallower water. I do not, of course, mean that such access is totally denied to the trout. We have all, when wading, had the experience of seeing trout rise nearer to the bank than we are standing; but generally speaking there will be fewer trout in shallows where there are wading anglers than there would otherwise have been, while the presence of these anglers also prevents boat anglers fishing these shallows.

Fortunately, the fact that on most days there are plenty of opportunities for boat anglers to catch trout from deeper water more than compensates. More often than not, the boat angler can catch his fish by one of three methods, all of which involve anchoring the boat. In my experience, it pays to anchor more often than not, but it is well at this stage to consider the exception—i.e., when it is better to drift.

This is when you expect the fish to be feeding at or near the surface but cannot decide where. That happens when there is a considerable wave, enough to prevent rises being observed, except at close range. In such conditions, trout are seldom found at great depths. Except perhaps in exceptionally cold conditions, they will be at or near the surface, and in the absence of any other clue to their whereabouts, the only way to find them is to drift.

Even then, it usually pays, as soon as a concentration of fish is located, to take the boat round and back past the fish, then drop downwind to within casting distance and anchor.

The same procedure is adopted when the water surface allows rises to be seen. Rising trout move upwind, just below the surface. They do not, however, pile themselves in heaps on the weather shore! What seems to happen is that they move upwind, feeding as they go, until the supply of whatever they are eating begins to peter out. They then turn and travel downwind at a depth of some 6–8ft, going very fast indeed, until they reach what, for want of a better term, we may call the downwind end of the food supply. There they turn again, come up to the top, and work upwind again. The speed at

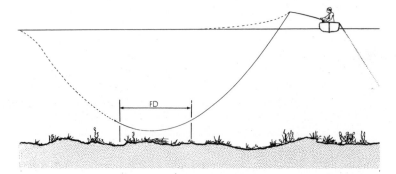

How a 30yd throw behaves in water 20ft deep. FD is the effective fishing distance

which they travel upwind, feeding, is probably determined by the density of the food supply.

This is a common pattern of trout behaviour, which I have often observed not only visually but with the aid of sonar equipment, the indications of which have led to my statement about trout going downwind fast at 6–8ft from the surface. You can see the return echoes flashing through the beam at this depth, while fish can also be seen moving upwind at the surface, and I am fairly sure that my ideas about the behaviour pattern are correct.

When trout are feeding like this, there seems to me to be no point at all in allowing a boat to drift. It will only drift out of the area in which the fish are feeding and have to be brought back again to the head of the drift. Every second that is occupied in bringing it back is fishing time wasted, quite apart from the fact that the disturbance caused may scare many of the trout and put them down.

If the boat is correctly positioned and anchored, there will be plenty of trout constantly moving upwind and coming within casting range, as long as the supply of food that is attracting them persists.

Two points arise from this. The trout that are returning from their upwind trip, going back at 6–8ft from the surface, are not feeding. Trying to interest them in flies or lures fished at that depth is a waste of time. I do not say that it will never catch a trout; I do say that in the time you spend doing it, many more fish could be caught by surface or near-surface flies. I might add that if a trout, going fast downwind at this depth, does take a fly that has been cast downwind, he will hit it with an almighty thump and you will be lucky indeed if you avoid a break. Much better to wait until that fish comes back just below the surface—it surely will.

The other point concerns etiquette. It is very naughty to cut into another boat's drift, as everyone knows; if, however, a boat is anchored at or near the upwind end of an area in which trout are feeding at the surface, its occupants cannot reasonably expect to hog the whole strip of water downwind of their position, right to the far side of the lake or reservoir!

In these circumstances it seems to me perfectly reasonable for another boat to anchor farther downwind, as long as a gap of 100yd or so is left. The second boat will be manned by some very clever anglers indeed if it succeeds in catching 5 per cent of the trout that

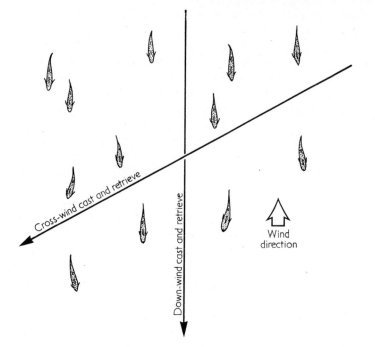

How a cast across the line of the wind will show the fly to many more surface-feeding fish than a downwind cast

pass it on their upwind trek! I remember vividly anchoring my boat at Hanningfield, with five other boats so positioned that upwind-moving trout had to pass all of them before they reached me; yet I had seven good fish in an hour and half, the other boats doing well at the same time.

So perhaps we may agree that the anchored boat should be treated by other boats exactly as a wading angler should be treated.

One more thing about trout feeding upwind. A fly moved across their line is much more likely to be taken than one cast straight downwind. You've only to examine an artificial wet fly to see why. It looks much more attractive from the side than from the rear! Even with dry flies, I think a cross-wind throw increases the likelihood of hooking fish soundly; and of course, a retrieve of any fly across the wind must bring it to the notice of far more fish than the retrieve straight upwind, in a direct line with the path the fish are taking.

So far, I have been talking about fish feeding at the surface, which, I repeat, can happen over water of any depth in reservoirs. If they are not at the top, they are usually really deep down. In hot weather, especially in the middle hours of the day, they are often 25–30ft down, and sometimes as deep as 40–50ft. The only way to catch trout at such depths with fly-fishing tackle is to anchor the boat and make a long cast with a fast-sinking line. The Hi-D line has a sinking rate of about 4in per second, so that after casting, it takes a full minute to sink 20ft. You need a stop-watch to do the job of timing the sinking allowance properly.

For effective fishing, your casting range ought to be at least three times the depth. The line sinks into a curve, so that by the time it reaches the fishing depth, it will be much nearer than the distance you cast. Your retrieve must necessarily be partly upwards. With a 30yd cast and a 20ft depth, you'll be lucky if your fly fishes as much as 10yd at the correct depth. Notwithstanding the difficulties, this deep fishing from an anchored boat can catch you fish in conditions where any other fly-fishing method would be quite useless. As an alternative to retrieving, you can try allowing the fly to lie inert on the bottom, a procedure that can be rather dull until the rod starts on its way over the side! That happens more often than most anglers are willing to believe.

Naturally, the choice of fly or lure and the method of fishing are important considerations, but more important still is the positioning of the angler or anglers correctly in relation to the fish, which are often in or over very deep water, and more often than not can be caught better from a boat that is anchored rather than one that drifts.

March 1971   *Richard Walker*

Sedges round the edges

I was recently visited by a friend from Edinburgh to whom I had promised a day on our local reservoir. An experienced fly fisher and competent fly dresser, with a lifetime's experience of fishing Scottish rivers and lochs, on only a few occasions had he tried his hand at reservoir rainbows. I had complete confidence in him, but must admit it suffered a blow when I asked to see his sedge-fly imitations.

'We seldom use them,' he said. 'If sedge ever show heavy on the water and the fish are on them, we usually find a March Brown or a Harelug does the trick. Anyway, if you leave out the Grannom, they're only a back-end bonus.'

I was astonished at this reply as well as reminded of the day, some years before, when I stood in John Veitch's shop in Peebles High Street trying to convince the old maestro of the importance of midges, particularly the pupa stage. John was a man who would tolerate no humbug, and in his view, at that time, relating midges to trout was humbug.

'I've nae time for them,' he bristled, 'and nayther hae the troots . . . and ony fisher that has must be gey glaiket.'

I never found out whether or not John subsequently changed his mind, but I did manage to convince my Edinburgh friend that as far as our local reservoir was concerned 'sedges round the edges' was no empty slogan, for we both secured limit bags by observing it, yet during our time at the water only a few sedge-flies were actually seen.

It is possible there are many other experienced river fly fishers who are inclined to neglect the sedges when fishing for stillwater rainbows, simply because their rough-stream training has not called for them to the same extent it has for upwinged flies. If there are, and like my friend they blanket sedges as merely a 'back-end bonus', they are being a bit naive.

Such a viewpoint can only be the result of assessing the sedge potential by the frequency and density of hatches actually seen, which seems to me a poor yardstick when one considers that many sedge hatches take place at night, so are not seen, and that most of the trout feeding is done on the larvae and pupae, also not seen. So, if there is a 'back-end' bonus, it can mean only the opportunity to fish the sedge dry. However, if a water is known to contain sedges, it seems to me to be folly for the angler to depend on and wait for a hatch when he could be exploiting the pupae successfully.

I have not always held that opinion, for I well remember a sheltered stretch of upper Tweed, opposite Easter Happrew farm, which was a favourite sedge area. Black silverhorns, grouse wings and browns flitted about the margins in small clouds and many a creel of spotted beauties came my way through fishing dry until the adult flies dispersed, an occurrence I accepted as the signal to move on. Since then, experience with sedge pupae has shown me how foolish I was to depart with the hatch, and I now know that a few before-and-after tactics with the pupae would almost certainly have added weight to my basket.

When it comes to dressing sedge pupae, I find a few liberties can be taken without detriment to the end result. Colour shades vary so much in the natural insects that I am convinced they are of secondary importance, and provided the general shade, after wetting, is reasonable, then movement, size and shape, probably in that order, are what matters. Of the two pupae dressings that have provided me with the most sport, the first has a body of teased orange wool mixed 50–50 with yellow seal fur, while the second has a similar mixture but with bottle-green wool instead of orange.

The wool, apart from influencing the shade of the pupa, helps to bind the seal fur when dubbing and absorbs water well enough to drag the pupa down to a depth suitable for manipulating. To give bulk and a taper shape I use a base of a single-ply from a piece of four-ply wool of a colour similar to that of the body, leaving a space near the hook eye for three or four turns of bronze peacock herl. The hackle is a short, stiffish ginger, plucked from near the throat of a cock cape.

Ribbing appears to be optional, for I have found the fish take the pupa with or without it, but in the latter case some pupae suffer disfigurement from the teeth of the trout, so a fine gilt wire ribbing may be added for protection. The rough body is scissor-trimmed after dressing to leave a bristly outline, and the best hook sizes I have found to be 10 and 12.

Fishing from the reservoir bank was most successful with two pupae to a leader, the size 10 on point and 12 on dropper. They fished equally well, according to conditions, on a floating line, sink-tip or slow-sinker, and the retrieve was similar with each line: cast

out, wait up ten seconds, and then start a slow, steady retrieve with
an occasional twitch and pause imparted at will. Takes were quite
positive and at times could be felt, but more success came from
visual concentration on the line with a quick and firm tightening at
the slightest indication of a draw.

Since sedges of one species or another keep revealing themselves
from early in the season to its end, there can be little doubt that sub-
surface trout activity among the larvae and pupae is almost
continuous. That in itself should be sufficient to indicate that fishing
sedges round the edges in the form of pupae is sensible practice
throughout the season, and dry-sedge fishing, exciting though it is,
must be relegated on its own to the position of 'back-end bonus'.

July 1976   *John Poole*

A last day to remember

Of all the many fishing days, the one that has, for me, the greatest
significance is the last day of the trout season. Whether it is that
some resurgence of optimism causes me to feel that the mistakes and
disappointments of the dying season will be offset by some
noteworthy achievement, I cannot say. All I know is that on that
particular day some force well-nigh irresistible draws me to reservoir
or river.

One such day had a special poignancy, because not only was it
the last day of the season, it was also almost certainly the last time I
would ever visit the little river near the Surrey/Hampshire border
that I had had the good fortune to fish for the past eight years.
Business called me back to the north; my house in Surrey was
already sold and in a few weeks' time my family and I would be on
the move again. Small wonder, then, that the call of the river was
particularly insistent and that I had so organised things that I would
be able to get in a couple of hours' fishing before going to the office.

It was one of those September days of rare beauty—hot,
cloudless and still—and the river was just about as unfishable as I

had ever seen it! The water was very low and clear and there were great islands and streamers of weed everywhere. As I made my way slowly upstream, occasionally essaying a perfunctory cast towards some likely lie, the peace and beauty of it all seemed to soak into my bones and charm away the tensions of recent weeks. It mattered little that no ring of a rising fish ruffled the smooth face of the river. Time passed . . .

I came to the place where a caravan stood in a field beside the stream. Nearby, I found three stout pegs driven in to the river bank; there was a night-line attached to each peg. The caravan was unoccupied, so I kicked the pegs loose and threw them into the bracken, having first pocketed the lines to remind me to call at the bailiff's cottage on the way up to town.

Time passed . . . but of trout there was no sign.

At one pool, where a capful of breeze momentarily ruffled the glassy surface, I managed to deceive a brace of careless grayling into taking my fly. But that was all. The September day burned slowly away and I was content. Soon—all too soon—I must be thinking of returning.

And then I saw it! Out in midstream, in a fast run between two beds of weed, lay a splendid trout—and it was feeding as though laying in a store of food for the winter. I couldn't see what the fish was taking, but every few seconds it rose, sipped some minute creature from the surface and sank back again. Up . . . sip . . . down . . . on and on, boldly and quite regardless of my crouching figure on the bank.

It was at once apparent that my somewhat limited casting abilities would need the support of a fair amount of luck if I were to put a fly over that trout. It was feeding just on the far side of an almost solid wall of weed, and between me and the weed the current ran smooth and strong. The instant my fly touched the water it was whisked away by the downstream drag on my line. Had it not been for our strict no-wading rule, I think I could have got into the river and put a fly over the fish fairly easily. As it was, the position seemed hopeless.

Nevertheless, I kept on trying, with my fly behaving more like a jet-propelled speedboat than a natural insect! And the extraordinary thing was that throughout the entire ham-fisted performance the big trout went on feeding. I had started casting in a kneeling position, but soon I was standing up and casting rather carelessly in what must have been full view of the trout had it deigned to acknowledge my existence.

Then, of course, the inevitable happened. I felt my fly touch something behind me, hesitated for a split second and then went through with the cast. The result was an absolute botch-up, with several coils of wet line descending with a splash on top of the weed and about a foot from where the trout lay.

'And that's the end of that little interlude,' I thought as I started reeling in.

I could see my Black Gnat floating among the tangled coils of cast and line, and, as I reeled in, that amazing trout literally shouldered its way over the weed, across two or three coils of line and daintily sucked in the tiny fly.

It seemed an age before the message from my brain started my limbs into action, but it was probably only a fraction of a second before I raised my rod high and simultaneously started cranking furiously at the reel and dashing backwards to try to get a tight line. But the fates that make sport of the efforts of anglers were only just warming to their work. I tripped neatly over a log lying in the long grass and went down with a truly stupefying crash.

I got up quite slowly and started reeling in again, quite sure by now that any contact there may have been between me and that trout had long since ceased. Then, suddenly, my rod slewed sideways and down, alarmingly, and about 15yd downstream something like 18in of trout leapt high in the air and fell back with a mighty splash.

I was still reeling in as the trout dashed back upstream. I had an excellent view of the fish as it passed within 4ft of me—yards of slack line trailing in the water—and before I could do anything about it, the trout had plunged deep into the weed. Convinced by now that I really had lost it, I tightened cautiously and gave a tentative tweak to the line with my left hand. The effect was as though a depth charge had exploded. Trout, water and weed flew high.

Straight downstream it went while I strove to bring the situation under some sort of control. For a few seconds I had the fish on a tight line and sawing from side to side, then it plunged away again into another weed-bed. This time it didn't even stop. The trout went through that weed like a torpedo and when it came out at the other side, my line, against all probability, was still with it and bedecked with weed like Monday's washing-line.

There was a deep, clear pool below the weed and there we fought it out for what seemed like an age. That trout just would not give up. Time and again it stood on its head and bored down and down, the rod bucking like a live thing in my hand. but at last the time came when I felt it was safe to unclip the landing net. The trout came slowly in, rolling now. I had one leg in the water and, as I slid the net out, I could clearly see my fly hooked into a tiny sliver of skin in the angle of the trout's jaws. And, even as I watched, the hook pulled out. I made a despairing lunge, and that blessed fish rolled over and swam slowly down into the folds of the net.

My hands were shaking as I gently laid the landing net down: it was some moments later that I realised my right gum-boot was full of water.

It was a beautiful fish—well over 2lb, probably close on 3lb, far and away the biggest I had ever seen taken from our water and, for all I knew, an all-time record for the river. It didn't flop about but just lay there across the folds of the net and looked at me with its bold, bright eye. And I know it sounds fanciful, but the look it gave me seemed to say quite clearly:

'Well, that was fun while it lasted, but you must admit that you were a trifle lucky. Anyway, it's your move now, Sir.'

So I picked up the fish across the palms of my hands and slid it gently into the water . . . And what did it all add up to in the end? Nothing much, really. Just that I went fishing on the last day of the season, caught a big trout and returned it to the river. And yet, so long as I draw breath, I will remember that fish.

January 1970   *Tom Atkinson*

Salmon

Salmon the leaper

It would be difficult to find a game angler who did not know that the salmon is called *Salmo salar*; but I am afraid it would be equally difficult to find one who knows what salar means. If you asked a Latin scholar he would tell you that the word is derived from a Latin verb meaning 'to jump or leap' and that 'salar' means 'leaper'.

If you happen to read ancient Gaelic myths, or hear them told, you will often find that when the hero is in a tight spot he overcomes his difficulty by doing a 'salmon leap', that is, an astounding jump. Both the scientist and the humble story-teller have been struck by the same peculiarity: the ability of the salmon to leap remarkable distances in difficult conditions.

Why do salmon jump? Quite simply, because they can and must. Other lively fish, such as trout and dace, do it as well, though in a less spectacular way, and for the same reasons.

The salmon and sea-trout are freshwater fish, which go down to the sea to seek the abundant food they cannot find in the clear mountain streams where they were born. But their eggs and young need, imperatively and unavoidably, cold, clear and well-oxygenated water. In consequence, the mature fish must go and spawn where such conditions exist, no matter how long and arduous the journey. You cannot argue with necessity, whether you are a man or a salmon.

Some biologists have advanced the theory that salmon must return to freshwater for another reason. In the sea the rich pastures make them big and fat; fat is lighter than muscle and a fat fish is more buoyant than a lean one. When the flesh of a salmon is saturated with oil, the fish becomes uncomfortably buoyant in the dense water of the sea and it then seeks freshwater where it can keep near the bottom with less effort. This may well be a contributory cause, possibly even a 'trigger' reaction preparatory to spawning; but it would not apply to the brown trout, which also seeks the small streams in the spawning season without ever having been to the sea.

What is incontestable is that the salmon leaving the sea and entering a river is a well-fed, fat and vigorous fish, capable of remarkable feats of strength, as any angler who has hooked one can tell (and will). If such a fish has to swim upstream towards the river's sources and finds an obstacle, such as a weir, waterfall or rapid, it has to go over it. It can swim against a rapid, taking occasional rests behind boulders, but it must jump over the weir or waterfall. Swimming against water cascading even a few feet would be almost impossible—the current is too strong—but air presents far less resistance. A flying-fish is a powerful swimmer, but when in danger it prefers to leap in the air and glide a long distance on its out-stretched pectoral fins: a short run and a long jump through the friendly air that offers so little resistance to its streamlined shape.

To make a high jump, a fish must take a fast run before sprinting into the air, and that is what the salmon does. It needs a pool with sufficient water, lying under the weir or waterfall; if that is not available, it will wait patiently for a rise in the level of the water, even if that rise is accompanied by an increase in the speed of the stream. That is why people passing over such a bridge as the Corrib at Galway often see the river below paved with salmon waiting for a chance to jump over the weir. Once the pool has sufficient water, the salmon can reach even in a small space a speed that gives it enough momentum to carry it several feet into the air and over the obstacle.

It is difficult, of course, to time the maximum speed of fish swimming in their element, where we cannot see well. Small wonder, therefore, if different observers have attributed different speeds to the salmon, from seven to twenty-four miles an hour. If anyone thinks that such speeds are unremarkable, let him remember that the athletic achievement of the four-minute mile is equivalent to a speed of fifteen miles an hour.

The salmon's speed is certainly sufficient to hurtle the fish in the air to a height of 8ft, and leave it with enough energy left to swim up through the rushing waters at the head of the waterfall. I know that the salmon has been credited with higher leaps than 8ft, but usually by people whose imagination was better than their capabilities for judging distance. It is preferable to stick to figures carefully observed and measured, especially as the salmon has collected round itself quite a wealth of legends and tall stories.

To quote one, there is still a widespread belief that the salmon leaps in a curve by bending itself and sprinting like a released spring. This is a completely mistaken idea, as many of my readers will confirm from personal observation or from seeing films of European or Pacific salmon leaping over waterfalls.

It has probably arisen from seeing a salmon (or a trout or pike, if it comes to that) jumping out of the water and turning, twisting, shaking its head in an attempt to free itself from the hook and line of the angler. Sometimes they may jump in the air and twist their bodies when chasing each other in play; but the classical salmon leap is a straight as an arrow and shimmering like silver. It is a beautiful, arresting sight that remains in the memory of the beholder as the most striking character of *Salmo salar*, Salmon the leaper.

September 1955   *A F Magri MacMahon*

The opening day

There are, I think, few more delightful feelings than to know that once again one stands on the threshold of a new salmon fishing season, that for the next seven or eight months the rivers will be open, and that whenever one has the time and inclination one may go fishing.

It is, of course, proverbial that so often anticipation is better than realisation and, alas, this is probably more true of fishing than most other sports. Hunting seasons, generally, do not vary greatly, except possibly in some years there is more frost and snow than in others. Much the same applies to shooting for the game bird situation is usually known fairly accurately before the season begins.

But with fishing everything lies in the lap of the gods, hidden in the mists of the future, because those two great unpredictables, the weather and the supplies of fish, can never be estimated or foretold. Some of the less wise, however, rush in where angels fear to tread, and attempt to do just that.

Yet history abounds with examples striking enough to show how foolish it is to suppose that because there were plenty of spawning fish and favourable weather in, say, the autumn of 1954, the prospects for 1959, when the main harvest of four-year olds is due to return, are excellent. Or that, after a year when salmon are scarce, we are likely to have poor fishing in five years' time.

To emphasise this I will give one instance of how wrong each type of forecast can be. The year 1929 was a poor one for salmon almost everywhere. In the Tamar-Tavy for example, the nets had only 358 salmon, by far the lowest total since records were kept and little more than 10 per cent of average. The rod catch of fifty-six was the lowest for at least the last fifty years. Yet 1934, when the small spring and summer fish were due to return, was one of great plenty. These same nets had 4,965, the second highest total ever. Rods did not share in the great harvest to the same extent because of a dry summer, the total being 272; but the fish were there all right.

Then take the reverse. In 1913 the Wye had a record catch of 9,946 salmon by rods and nets. Yet in 1918 the spring run was no better than average, and was followed by the total failure of the summer fish to return, although, as it was during World War I, the nets were kept on until 31 August, instead of stopping on 15 August.

Sometimes one is inclined to wish to see into the future and to know what is going to happen in the weeks and months ahead. But I don't think I should ever want to do this where salmon fishing is concerned. While the unknown is still unknown, hope springs eternal. But that hope could hardly have survived had I known on the opening day in February 1956, that the rainfall here for the four months February, March, April and May would be no more than 5.65in compared with an average of 15.67in, and in all that time I should go to the river but thrice for a total of six hours' fishing; and that not until 5 June would I hook my first salmon for the season. Truly in this case ignorance, if not exactly bliss, was a good deal less shattering than knowledge would have been.

And when the great day really does arrive what are one's main reactions? First, I am sure, is the feeling of pleasure to be fishing again after the long winter months. Second, probably, is to note the changes that spates have made in the pools. Not all of these may be easy to judge now if the water is high, but in a rain-fed, fast river, few opening days find all the pools the same shape and depth as one left them in October.

Then there is the eternal query 'clean or kelt?' when one feels the first heavy pull, which sends a thrill of excitement down one's spine and makes the knees tremble. I can agree with Chaytor when he says that he welcomed a kelt on the first day of a new season, 'when,' as he writes, 'a pull of any kind gives you a jump of pleasure'.

But if the playing of a strong lively kelt is a pleasure, the unhooking of it can be an operation of quite considerable pain. How seldom one seems to lose kelts and how rarely are they lightly hooked in the front or near the outside of the jaw where it is easy to get at the hook!

A kelt's teeth are like tiny razors, and when the fish will not lie still the releasing of a treble far back in the mouth is a minor version of the notorious Chinese torture, 'the death of a thousand cuts'. In difficult cases it will save time and pain, the first important for the fish, the second for oneself, to keep the mouth open with an improvised gag made from a short piece of stick; and also to have handy a disgorger.

And if fortune smiles and one does hook a 'right un', which is seen early in the battle to be the real thing, one lives and dies a hundred times before the end comes. And then either one looks upon the gleaming prize with that feeling of intense exaltation that only a salmon can bring, or, if the luck has been bad, remembers sadly the words of Robert W Service: 'You felt that your life had been looted clean of all it once held dear.'

February 1957   *Kenneth Dawson*

My first fish

It was a fine June morning with light, high clouds dusting a blue sky and the sun occasionally peeping through. I was staying at a small but comfortable riverside hotel on the Exe and had been fly fishing for trout with reasonable success, and fly fishing and spinning for salmon with no success, for two days.

The previous evening a fellow-angler had told me that he had seen a salmon turn over downriver. 'There's a trout pool,' he said, 'and a bit further down the river deepens into a run between a rock bed and runs out into deeper water with back eddies under the far bank.'

I mentioned this to the landlord's son who told he that this was, indeed, the best salmon pool on their stretch of the river. 'Down by that tree with roots growing out into the water. But mind,' he cautioned, 'it's hard to drop a spinner in the right place, and besides, we haven't had a salmon taken since March.'

When I walked out of the hotel on to the fine lawns at nine o'clock there was a man with a young lad already wet-fly fishing in the foam and spray tumbling under the ancient bridge. The lad hooked and landed a trout while I watched.

'Already had two,' said his companion. 'Pheasant Tail. Plenty of room for you.'

I thanked him and shook my head. 'I'm told there's a salmon about and I'd like to have a go.'

They bade me good luck, and I pulled on my waders, collected my gear and, with my seven-year-old son beside me, walked off down the river bank watching the swirls and eddies over a bed that varied between rocks and silt. I could see that the level had fallen a few inches overnight and the water was clearing fast.

We approached the pool with caution, keeping high up on the bank, and I sat looking at the target spot for several minutes before tackling up. I had a 9ft glass-fibre spinning rod and a fixed-spool reel loaded with 11lb line. I chose to fish a 2in blue devon.

The cast was a difficult one beneath spreading branches low over the pool, but after two or three tentative throws I got the length right and the devon acted beautifully back to me, but too shallow by far in the water. Taking a chance, I squeezed on a swan shot about 1ft up the line and cast again. I snagged on the retrieve, but fortunately recovered everything and decided against taking off the shot for something lighter.

The next cast was a beauty—one of those that give pleasure even if you don't take a fish, with the spinner landing almost without splash in exactly the right place. I let the line run out a yard or two before applying the bale arm, and then watched with satisfaction as the line cut across the water. At about mid-stream and 20yd down I was snagged again in the same place as before. I cursed silently and watched for a moment or two, then the line started moving again, back towards the pool under the far bank.

I suppose I was paralysed for no more than two seconds as the truth dawned; then I raised the rod slightly and felt the resistance as the line continued across to the pool. I dared not let the fish sound under those spreading branches and I struck hard and firm.

Immediately the line screamed off the reel and I thanked God I had remembered to adjust the clutch before starting.

My son leapt to his feet. 'What is it, Dad?' he yelled. 'A big trout, I think,' I panted, not daring to believe that I really had hooked the king of the river. And then, at an unbelievable distance downstream, that beautiful, that magnificent, that breath-taking fish broke surface in a mighty bound. Rainbows rippled across the silvered, arching back, diamond droplets of water scattered across the surface as the fish thrashed back into the depths.

'Salmon!' we both screamed and the fight was on.

Who can describe the sight of that first salmon on the hook, the disbelief that any fish can exert so much pressure, the sinking feeling that it just will not be possible ever to get that leaping, twisting, sounding torpedo of muscle out of the water and on to the bank. I remember thinking that I did not have the experience or know-how to land that fish, but I tried to recall every fishing experience I had ever heard or read about. Meantime, the fish was trying with every sinew to make off with all my line, heading downsteam as though only sight of the sea would stop him.

I raised the rod as high as I dared and watched the quivering bow with apprehension. I tightened the clutch slightly and hung on. At last the run stopped, but I made no attempt to recover line until I felt slack, and then it was an inch-by-inch job. Three times I got the fish back towards me, each time closer, each time nearer the surface, and each time the rush to escape was shorter.

Eventually, I got the fish level with me at mid-stream and it swam in towards me while I turned the handle slowly and cautiously.

When the fish was under the bank it sounded in 6ft of water, and there it skulked sullenly. I held the line taut, feeling every ounce of quivering muscle as the fish strove to stay down. For a moment I felt remorse at the thought of that free and fearless fish now captive. But now the line began to move again and I reeled in to see my quarry faintly beneath the surface. Alas, it saw me too, and with one last valiant effort threw itself thrashing back to mid-stream. There it surfaced, spent, on its side, and as I reeled firmly in I realised with horror that my small trout net would not nearly encompass this splendid and apparently enormous creature.

'I'll have to bank it,' I thought, 'but the bank's too steep. I'll have to handline it.' And by this time all the 'have to's' were too late. The fish was floating right under my nose. Keeping the line tight, I laid the rod on the bank.

'Hold the line tight, Andrew,' I instructed my son, 'and don't pull on it. Just keep it tight.'

While he did so, I kneeled and ran my hand down the line, into the water and gently drew the salmon to me. Throwing caution to the winds, I suddenly heaved the fish out of the water on to the bank and fell on it—bodily. The heavenly shades of former Exe salmon fishermen must have shuddered in horror, but I cared not. I had my beautiful fish, safe and sound.

It was a hen-fish, fresh-run and clean as a sliver of sea ice. Back at the hotel and under the admiring eyes of the trout anglers we weighed her in at 10lb 9oz. Photographs were taken to be kept and treasured, as was the kiss of one of the waitresses, who seemed even more thrilled than I at such a fine fish.

'I'll clean it out, wrap it in foil and put it in the deep-freeze for you,' said the chef.

'Daddy, please don't do that,' my son implored. 'I want it stuffed and I want it on the wall in my bedroom.'

But to me that fish was neither eaten nor stuffed, nor is it really no longer alive. No other fish I have ever caught, and there have been many, compares with that first salmon. Over and over again I have re-lived those thrilling moments. In times of stress I have seen again those rainbow leaps. Struggling for sleep, I have felt the rod arch and the fish fight and the dank, dark reedy, watery smell of the river touches my nostrils with remote magic that brings peace and sometimes even tranquillity.

How is it that what is apparently so trivial an incident against the vast and stormy canvas of life's vicissitudes can have had such a lasting effect on an individual?

Anglers will all understand and so, I believe, will others whose moments of joy have been crystallised in the soaring flight of an eagle, the leap of a deer or even the satisfying plunk of a golf ball dropping after a long and almost miraculous putt.

Emotional turmoils that, at the time, threatened to engulf and even destroy me, now often seem remote and stupid, but as long as I live so will that first salmon.

November 1973   *Philip Nathan*

Don't stick to one style in the spring

The term 'spring salmon' loosely defines those fish that enter our rivers any time between early January and late May. They are an unpredictable lot, for they can vary in size from the small Tweed fish to the monsters of the Eden, Avon and Wye. The fish of some rivers seem to have little in common with those of other rivers and the mystery why there should be such a difference in size is still to be resolved.

If spring salmon vary greatly in their size, however, they do not vary greatly in habits, and those small, fit fish of the Tweed are just as likely to take the same bait or fly as the monsters of the Avon or Wye. Troubles arise in the tactics we adopt for catching spring fish from various rivers, for the techniques that might work well on, say, the Tweed, might not even produce an offer on the Avon.

In general, early-spring fishing means using a double-handed spinning rod with a multiplying or fixed-spool reel and line of suitable strength (normally not less than 12lb test). Big baits are frequently required during the early months and it is a question of fishing them as slowly and as deeply as possible. On rivers like the Avon it may be a matter of slowly searching out narrow runs between weedbeds, whereas the Tweed and Tay will call for greater assessment of current depth and strength to choose a bait of suitable weight.

In general I am opposed to the use of additional lead weighting and feel that if extra weight is required it should be in the bait itself. The time for British bait manufacturers to provide us with a greater range of weights of baits seems long overdue. At the moment the only way the angler can vary the weight of a bait is to have a selection made in different materials. Thus a $2\frac{1}{2}$in metal devon minnow could be selected in place of a $2\frac{1}{2}$in plastic devon minnow if extra weight is required. There are numerous occasions when I would like to stay with a certain size of bait, but would like to have them in varying weights. At the moment this can only be done in the way I have outlined.

Additional lead weighting, of course, has to be used at times, but I do not like it and would rather have all the weight required in the bait itself. For early-spring fishing, however, I think it is impossible to over-emphasise the need for the bait to swim slow and deep. Much the same applies if the angler prefers fly fishing, and the flies selected should be just as long and heavy as any spinning bait (rarely less than 2in) and be fished from a long rod and a sinking line.

With either type of fishing, be it fly or bait, it is essential to make fairly long casts to get the lure down. The rod should be held well out over the water, with its tip well up in the air, if the lure is to sink deeply enough. If the weight for the spinning bait has been correctly assessed, there should be little or no necessity to wind the reel handle during the period when the bait is moving through the likely portion of the stream—unless the current is exceptionally sluggish. Failure to appreciate this slow movement causes most failure during the early months.

As the mantle of winter falls away from the land and the first dawn choruses jingle our senses into the reality of spring, many anglers begin to wonder what is the precise time to change from spinning to greased-line fly fishing. There may well be a lengthy period of transition, when the salmon will accept anything from a thundering big spoon to a small fly. For many of us this can be a difficult period. It is so easy to carry on spinning too long when the fish are losing interest in this bait, and it is just as easy to make an early switch to greased-line fishing before the fish are fully conditioned to take the sub-surface lure.

My own remedy lies in the use of medium-sized flies on a floating line with a sinking tip. The fly is presented more easily at a mid-water depth, is still sufficiently large to evoke interest from deep-lying salmon, but not so large or so small and near the surface that it will either frighten the deep-lying fish or fail to offer sufficient inducement for them to rise to the surface for it. Flies should rarely be smaller than a No.4 and not much bigger than a $1\frac{1}{2}$in tube.

Fishing with this type of outfit has taken a lot of guesswork out of 'transition-period' fishing and has frequently produced good bags for me when spinners and greased-liners are hovering on the brink of change. Its success will depend to a great extent on the type of water to be fished, but in this transition period it has proved effective with both deep-lying and running salmon.

By the time water temperatures have moved steadily and permanently into the low fifties there should be little doubt about the merits of real greased-line fishing, particularly when water levels are settled and there has been no irritating up-and-down action following melting snow or heavy rain; it is generally the month of May, with all of nature's loveliness in full blossom. The salmon then comes into that playful mood when it will take our flies near the surface and, if conditions are good, give us some great sport.

Most of my best greased-line fishing has frequently followed a rise in the water and has been preceded by good spinning conditions. Fresh fish have come into the beat and, as the water fines off, they settle in the pools and frequently take the fly well. A No.6 fly is generally considered the basic size and, until the water has dropped quite appreciably, I rarely bother to fish with anything smaller. Later, of course, the angler may well have to go to No.8s or even No.10s, but there should rarely be any reason to go smaller than this.

Pattern of fly is something that does not concern me greatly. The old standbys like Blue Charm, Logie, Thunder and Lightning, and Stoat's Tail have all stood the test of time.

Even with the advent of May and good greased-line conditions, it is a mistake to think that good sport with this method is bound to follow for the rest of the season. I recall many days when I have been glad to resort to a sinking line and small flies, or even small devon minnows on a spinning rod. Only long experience on one piece of water will indicate the best methods for a given day. The precise height of the water is another factor that has great influence upon the angler's chances. So it pays not to become too wedded to one style of fishing.

Spring fishing, therefore, may well mean fishing with anything from a 3in devon minnow, a spoon or natural sprat, to a small, lightly-dressed No.8 greased-line fly. It represents all that is best in salmon fishing, for the fish are fresh and in prime condition. The period covers a wide range of climatic conditions but can be rewarding for the angler with access to good water and the know-how to tackle the problem on a given day.

March 1970   *Arthur Oglesby*

Tactics for the summer

Faced with writing something about fishing in summer for salmon, I realise of course that the subject is one more than usually difficult adequately to deal with in brief: if for no other reason than that so much depends, at that time of year, upon the part of the country in which one is.

To fish a spate river on the west coast of Scotland or in Ireland may well be an entirely different proposition to flogging the Wye. Again, there are rivers in which salmon angling more or less tails off by the end of June and which boast no summer run. In other words, sport may be not only a matter of weather and water, but of stale or fresh fish also.

Nevertheless, summer, in the main, is small-fly time or, with the spinning rod, prawn and shrimp time, although there are always exceptions. One comes readily to mind from the River Nore in County Wexford, Eire.

Fishing there one August morning in dead low water and bright sun, despite the fact that I had not seen a fish for days, I felt convinced that one particular, shrunken, stream in the beat must hold a salmon. There was nothing, of course, other than wishful thinking, to support this supposition.

Having risen betimes—and so often the early hours and the 'dimmits' of late evening offer the best chances at that time of year—I went to work with copy-book methods and precision. Light tackle, small flies, great stealth and so on, however, proved of no avail. Not a thing stirred. Then in defiance of convention I threw the rule book to the winds. Changing to a heavier cast and tying on the biggest fly my box had to offer (a gaudy 2/0 confection somehow left behind from early spring) I was within minutes into a fish—albeit a small but very game and perfectly shaped cock. One just never knows with salmon fishing, and in the sticky conditions that are so often the order in summer, it may pay well to adopt the unorthodox. Similarly, resorting to a light, fat-bellied wooden minnow, spun fast up and across stream, can sometimes do the trick. By the same token a meticulously mounted brown shrimp worked down and across any likely water is frequently quite deadly.

In summer fishing it is worthwhile remembering that, with shrunken water and rich weed growth, salmon will take up and occupy all kinds of unexpected positions, deserting those well favoured and better known in spring and autumn. They choose the shallow, streamy and best aerated parts of the river, maybe where a bed of weed affords not only shade and cover, but a pleasant and life-sustaining oxygenated place in which to lie. These and all likely stickles deep enough to hold a fish should be carefully explored and will many a time bring reward.

I learnt, again in Ireland long ago, another warm water salmon expedient: invaluable advice given me one night in the local by an ancient, retired water bailiff. Having bemoaned to him my singular lack of success in the unpropitious conditions then prevailing, he gave me counsel that I put successfully into practice the very next morning. 'Go you, Sorr,' said he, 'to the river by darkness when the white misties lie low on the water and have your fly, or bait, ready for action by the time the first of the birds tune their voices. Start fishing as soon as the mistie, with the coming of the sun, begins smoking off the surface for it is then—if only for ten minutes—that you'll be after having him kilt. Himself, lying on the bottom for the rest of the day, will take for a while.'

I did as he bid and for three mornings in succession killed my fish, for everything happened just as he had said. Where, during the long hours of full daylight the river had for a week and more appeared empty, fish rolled up to the surface, but, directly the mist had evaporated, they as mysteriously vanished again from sight. The fourth morning proved only a blank; there was no mist and the river might have been utterly devoid of fish—not a single one showed anywhere. I have tried this method on other rivers and, conditions being right, have seldom known it to fail.

It may well be wise, in times such as the above, to confine one's energies to fishing early and late and make up lost sleep during daylight, for those summer nights are exceedingly short, especially if one has fished on into the dark. Flogging away during the hours of hot sunshine and cloudless skies is seldom rewarding, dulls concentration and patience (two essentials to good angling) and, more than possibly, disturbs and still further puts off what fish are present. They grow used to, and become tired of, the long succession of flies and baits continually shown to them. Most of us are too inclined, I think, to expect unreasonable behaviour on the part of our quarry and to overlook that the salmon is a creature of the wild, imbued with nature's instincts for self-preservation.

Another *sine qua non* of summer salmon fishing (although applicable to any time of the season) is to watch for, and take advantage of, all and every weather change; a rise or fall of barometric pressure, an acute change in wind may well—who knows why—bring on the golden moment of take. By the same token every endeavour should be made to be at the waterside for the 'first of the rise' following a downpour of rain or a storm in the hills. Stale and sluggish salmon will sense the coming of fresh water long before we humans do and, as the river at last begins to rise, the urge for adventure and movement stirs again with them and the first half hour or so (if not a swift rise) may result in a real killing. Once the river is 'away', however, and fish are on the move upstream, the chance has gone. Then all one can do is to wait for the water to subside and clear, and for any newcomers from the reaches below to settle down in their new positions. After that there may well be a further period for action.

Summer fishing can be disappointing but it can also, given a little luck in the shape of some fresh water at the right time, be great fun indeed.

June 1957   *Coombe Richards*

Now for the bright back-enders

With the passing of summer, most salmon rivers worthy of the name should have abundant stocks of fish, assuming that high-seas, netting, pollution, continued low water, or a host of other factors have not intervened to influence spring and summer runs. Indeed, with the resting leaf and the general decay of nature's loveliness, there will be many anglers who will lay their tackle aside in the sure knowledge that the best of sport is over.

There is little serious fishing fun in catching red and ripe stale salmon, and the thoughtful angler prefers to leave such fish to fulfil the more useful task of spawning. These fish will still have many trials ahead and may yet have to face a further onslaught of disease, privation and hardship before their task is completed. Such autumn fishing for stale fish does not come within the scope of this article.

There is a tendency, however, to think that all autumn fishing is for the stale spring and summer fish. But there are some rivers, notably the Tweed, that have a run of genuine autumn fish, and where fishing can not only be sporting (in the best sense of the word) but can also offer the chance of better-than-average-sized fish. Throughout spring and summer, when the earlier run fish may be suffering from lack of food, oxygen and healthy environment, the genuine autumn fish is still way out at sea, having last-minute snacks in the warm salt waters and getting itself into full fighting trim to face the rigours of spawning and winter. Admittedly, there may be some development of the gonads and ovaries, but such fish are worthy adversaries for the fortunate angler.

For many years now I have been lucky enough to have access to a stretch of the lower Tweed near Kelso. The season there does not finish until the end of November, and it is my custom to pick the last week of the season as being the most likely time when the big back-enders will run the river, though they may well come up any time from September onwards, depending on their whims and the state of the water.

There will also be quite a few fish that will not run the river until the season has closed, and I have often speculated on the possibility of the really big fish doing exactly this and being back at sea, spawning completed, before the new season opens. Suffice it to say that some of the really prime fish may be taken any time from September onwards, and if I can catch a genuine fresh-run autumn fish I regard it as good a sporting fish as any springer—and almost as good on the table.

Techniques of fishing for autumn fish have to be varied appreciably, depending on weather and water. During September the greased-line fly may fulfil most needs. Fly sizes may be varied according to water height and temperature, and towards the end of the month there may be days when a sinking line will bring better results. However, just as the spring fisher looks for all the signs of the zodiac to tell him when to quit spinning in favour of fly fishing, so the autumn angler should be ever watchful for the time to make a change back to spinning.

Certainly by the time October is past, there will be little point in continuing with the greased-line or sub-surface fly. But if fly fishing is mandatory, as it is on Tweed at this time, it will pay him to resort to the big tube flies on a sinking line. I have no doubt, however, that, where it is permitted, the spinner is the more effective lure, with sizes varied to suit conditions until, in the dying days of November, we are back using the same big spinners we would use in the early spring.

Another feature of late-November fishing is the distinct possibility of hooking a fresh-run springer—a fish that has run the river slightly earlier than its brothers, being two or three months ahead of its time. It has happened to me on more than one occasion, and a valued bonus such fish make. Generally, however, the angler is more likely to be troubled by the stale spring and summer fish, but in the lower reaches of the Tweed this is less likely to happen than higher upstream. Nowadays, if a fish is well developed with spawn, particularly a hen fish, I have no hesitation in removing the hook and popping the fish back into the river. It is useless as food and will accomplish a more worthwhile task if left to spawn, particularly in these days when salmon have to suffer so much from the hands of man.

Autumn fishing tactics are little different from those of any other time. The fly or bait is cast and fished in much the same way as in the spring, and the choice of size and bait or fly is governed by the same factors that would influence the choice at other times.

As in all types of salmon fishing, the height of the water will be a paramount consideration. It may well make the difference between a good day or a blank. It the water is on the big side and not too cold, it is a safe bet that the autumn fish will travel fast and far. But a few overnight frosts will slow down the run and hold the fish in the lower reaches for rather longer. There will then be times of day when fish will take well, and there will be little to beat a slow-spun spinner or a big fly fished slowly on a sinking line.

My own special technique for the Tweed in the dying months is to use a 2–3in fly tied on a brass tube. The fly may be garish or sombre, depending on the clarity and temperature of the water. For casting, I use a 14–15ft rod with a shooting portion of Hi-D WetCel line. some 12yd long, spliced to heavy monofil backing. A No.10 WetCel head is usually adequate for the rod described and enables the fly to get well down to the fish. Long casting is an advantage in this respect, but it is a simple matter to cast 25–30yd with the equipment I have described.

In the later weeks the fly should be fished as slowly as possible. The take from the salmon may well be lazy and log-like, and there will seem to be little difference from getting hung up on a rock. But it may well be as big a fish as you have encountered throughout the season and, if fresh-run, will contest the odds every inch to the bank. It will gleam like a deep bar of silver and sea-lice may well be still on it. Fish like this are the real autumn fish, the fish worth trying for and tussling with. They are a match for any salmon at any time of the year and represent the only autumn fishing the real sportsman should undertake.

October 1970   *Arthur Oglesby*

When salmon cease to feed

Opinions on the nature and extent of the feeding of adult salmon while in freshwater have been put forward at fairly regular intervals over the years. That it has been established beyond doubt that the salmon does not feed on its return to the river appears to have escaped the attention of many of those who have advanced theories to explain the food occasionally found in a salmon's stomach and why a salmon takes an angler's fly, lure or bait.

To some extent this is understandable because the results of the original investigations into the freshwater diet of the adult salmon were published around the turn of the nineteenth century in scientific journals that are not available today. Therefore, it might help to clear up any misunderstanding if the results of these investigations were summarised.

The first serious investigations into the freshwater diet of the salmon were carried out on the Rhine. Hoek examined 2,000 salmon from the lower Rhine and found food remains in the stomachs of only seven fish. Meischer Ruesch then examined 2,162 salmon caught over a period of four years at Basle, 500 miles further upstream, and found food in the stomachs of only two salmon, both kelts.

In this country, in 1894 and 1895, Tosh examined the stomach contents of 1,694 salmon from the Tweed. Of these, 1,142 were caught near to the estuary and 252 were taken some thirty miles upstream near Kelso. Of the former group (estuary caught fish), 128 (9.5 per cent) contained recognisable food, much of it of marine origin. Of the latter group, all the stomachs were empty. Paton also examined Tweed salmon and found no traces of food in the stomachs or intestines of 104 fish.

It can be seen from these results that only a few of the large numbers of salmon examined contained any food whatsoever. Many of these fish had eaten this food while they were still in the sea. Only a small proportion of the fish with food in their stomachs had actually ingested it while they were in the river. It is, therefore, quite clear from this evidence that the salmon does not feed while in freshwater.

Some confusion has arisen in the past about what is meant by the term 'feeding' and this requires definition in this context. Paton used the term to mean 'not the mere swallowing of material but the digestion, absorption and utilisation of the material by the body'. He also pointed out: 'That salmon take a fly, minnow or other shining object in the mouth is no argument as to their feeding in this sense. That they may, and occasionally do, take and swallow worms and other wriggling objects is well known. But the swallowing of a few worms can do but little to make good the enormous changes going on in the fish, even if, when swallowed, they are digested and used.'

Angling literature can provide many examples of the various items of food found in salmons' stomachs. Among them can be listed trout, elvers, eels, carp, dace, gudgeon, tench and many more types of invertebrates. However, when food does occur in a salmon's stomach, it usually consists of only one or two animals, and feeding cannot, in any way, be described as either extensive or varied. The food value of these items to the fish must be small indeed!

While in the sea the salmon feeds voraciously, building up enormous reserves of food. By the time it has returned to the river and entered the estuary it has usually ceased feeding altogether and contains little or no marine food in its stomach. While in the river it exists solely by drawing upon the reserves of food laid down while in the sea, taking no further nourishment from the river. This period of fasting may last from between only a few weeks to almost an entire year, depending upon the time when the fish entered the river.

During this period the food reserves are used to provide materials for the growth and maturation of the ovaries or testes, and to afford the often tremendous amounts of energy required to ascend the river to the spawning grounds. During the salmon's time in the river, the material stored in the muscles is gradually depleted, and there is absolutely no evidence that this loss is made good by fresh material taken in as food while in the river. Thus, the food value per unit of weight of the salmon decreases as the season advances. Paton stated that the food value of a fish caught in the upper waters of the river in October and November was about one-third of that of a fish caught in the estuary.

The often protracted fast of the salmon in freshwater is not without precedent. Many fish and higher animals that congregate within restricted areas to breed, limit or curtail their feeding activities. Biologically, there is good reason for this. It prevents all the available food within the area being severely depleted and thus ensures that sufficient food will be available for the young. The entire fish population of a salmon river would soon cease to exist if the salmon were to feed as voraciously in the river as they do in the sea.

Many theories have been advanced to explain the capture of a salmon with food in its stomach. Whatever the cause, it certainly does not result from the requirement to feed in the normal sense of this word. Explanations must be based upon some other motivation not associated with feeding; possibly curiosity, play or anger; perhaps the chance release of a normally supressed reflex activity; or some other activity, brought on by the chance combination of environmental stimuli and the appropriate physiological condition in the fish—i.e., the salmon 'forgets' that it is not supposed to feed.

One popular view is that the taking of food or other articles into the mouth by a salmon may represent no more than 'curiosity' in the fish. Apart from a developed sense of smell, the salmon also has an acute sense of touch, and it is suggested that the mouthing of an article represents the salmon's way of feeling and identifying it to satisfy this sense of curiosity, rather in the same way that a baby will take a new or unfamiliar article into its mouth and then, having satisfied its sense of curiosity, will reject the article. Even in adult life, the first action of many people when presented with a new or interesting article is to reach out to touch it. The salmon has no other means of touching an article, and so uses its mouth.

I doubt if a satisfactory scientific explanation to this question will ever be found, and such theories will always be based upon supposition. The important thing, as far as an angler is concerned, is not why a salmon takes an angler's fly, lure or bait, but the fact that it does so.

March 1972   *Graeme Harris*

Find a taking fish

One of the greatest attributes an angler can have when he is visiting a strange river is the ability to read the water and, from the character of its currents and contours, deduce where the salmon are likely to be lying.

Most of us have to fish a fair amount of unproductive water to find out where the taking places are. However, there are a few general principles applicable to most rivers that will, if properly applied, aid us in locating the lies on a strange water.

Salmon sometimes show in swirling and boiling water, but they seldom take in such situations, although in many instances such water seems attractive to the angler. The swirling currents make for instability and are not places in which the fish will find a comfortable lie. In contrast, they do seem to like places where the current is uniform, even if it is over a distance of only a few yards. This is especially so where there is a 'draw' on the water—which means the flow at the surface is markedly faster than that beneath. A rock ledge or a gravel shelf will cause this draw, as the water must necessarily flow more quickly over such an obstruction.

The same will happen to water flowing around a rock, or at the end of an obstruction that juts out from the bank. There is always a current gradient in flowing water, as the bed of the river slows the water in its vicinity, while that at the surface is unimpeded. The more marked this current gradient is, the more the salmon seem to like it. It is as though they like a really good flow of water over their backs, with an ease in the water about their bellies. Shallow depressions in the river bed, rock ledges and large stones help to create such conditions, and are consequently often good taking places.

For many years I've believed that salmon tend to lie behind rocks and boulders. Well, so they do, but experience has taught me that many more lie in front of such obstructions, and they tend to be taking fish. When the water hits a rock on the river bed it gets dammed up in front of it, while that on the surface accelerates over the obstruction. Thus there is an ease in the current at the level of the rock, with a sharply increasing speed gradient up to the surface water—and these are ideal conditions for a salmon lie.

If the rock is protruding from the water, the accelerating flow is around its sides. The current immediately behind the rock is then swirling and boiling in character, often with a build-up of sand and silt. Salmon do not usually lie over sand, so the area immediately behind the rock is unlikely to be productive. However, some yards below the obstruction and to its sides, there is usually an even accelerating flow that may form a good lie.

The depth of the water is a fundamental factor, and must be adequate. At least 3–4ft is usually needed to harbour a fish, but in the height of summer salmon may lie in shallower water, and grilse especially may be found in thin streamy areas in the throats of the pools. Presumably they favour such shallow tumbling water for its high oxygen content. In such conditions wading can easily be overdone, to the detriment of the day's fishing.

In the early spring, when the water is still cold (less than 45°F), salmon lie in the slacker water at the edges of the main current and towards the tails of the pools, but still in areas where there is a 'draw' on the water. As the temperature rises in late spring and early summer, the frequented lies are found in the main current and the upper parts of the pools.

As autumn approaches, and the later fish come in, there is a tendency for the fish to lie once again in the slacker water. As the temperatures drop later in the season, the fish no longer frequent the fast, oxygenated water that is their habitat during the heat of the summer. The autumn lies are often the same as the spring lies.

In times of flood, when the current is running fast and heavy throughout the pool, the easier water close in to the bank provides the only places likely to be productive. New points and obstructions will now be covered, and form new taking places. Much of the pool may be unfishable and short casts are more likely to be rewarding than longer casts into the central torrent, where one's lure will be swept away so rapidly that any salmon brave enough to be lying there will not have a chance of seeing it. Salmon tend to run in high water and the easier current near the bank is often the route they use.

After a flood, as the water is fining down but is still above normal height, the salmon continue to run, and this can be one of the most tantalising times of all for the angler. One sees fish showing all over the river but usually cannot get them to take. The locals will know where the resting lies are, but the visitor is often at a loss and can cover only those places he thinks are likely to hold a resting fish. Running fish seldom seem to take, but resting fish certainly do. If one is lucky enough to locate a resting lie by catching a fish, it is a sound idea to continue at the spot in the hope that another salmon will drop in.

On the more expensive waters the services of a gillie are a decided advantage and he will tell the tenant where the taking places are. It would be a brave man indeed (or a foolish one) who went in the face of such experienced advice—at least at first. If the usual places are unproductive, it may be interesting to back your own fancy. Many gillies are rather conservative in trying water that is not usually fished, and one is often greeted with the remark: 'That bit is never fished, sir. There are no lies.'

Nine times out of ten the gillie is right, but I am always left with the nagging feeling that water cannot be productive if it is never fished. So, on occasions, when the recommended lies have drawn a blank, try the water 'that is never fished', despite the disapproving looks from your gillie. You might—once in twenty years—prove him wrong by finding a new lie. Your name will then be indelibly written into the history of the river!

The ability to read water can come only with experience and by careful analysis of those places from which you have taken a fish. Note the water height, for it is certainly of importance, and then go back and study the area and the characteristics of the currents that constitute the lie.

Sometimes it is quite difficult to decide just where the take occurred, for in the excitement of hooking a salmon you are not likely to notice exactly where you were standing. When you do have a fish on it helps to glance round at the bank and make a mental note of a landmark that will enable you to return to exactly the same spot. Then, by casting about the same length of line you were using when you hooked the fish, you will be able to locate the lie to within a foot or so. You can build up a mental impression of the various types of lie in this way, and that knowledge will be an invaluable aid when you fish a strange river.

March 1972   *Alastair Perry*

The height of the water must be right

The successful salmon angler could be said to be one who is thoroughly versed in all legitimate methods of fishing for them. He will know his greased-line techniques, will have mastered spinning under all conditions and, if he is not content to go home fishless on occasions, he will also have those three aces up his sleeve: prawning, shrimping and worming—even if, like me, he resorts to them only out of dire necessity. Occasions, perhaps, when a film cameraman lurks in the background, urgently wanting footage of a fish being landed, or when unexpected guests wish for fresh salmon on the menu.

While, therefore, I mainly restrict my salmon fishing to the fly and spinner, there have been occasions when I have been glad of an alternative. Perhaps the most notable occasion to spring to mind was on the dark turbulent waters of Norway's Vosso river during June 1966, when, in desperation, a sink-and-draw prawn brought me my best salmon, a magnificent fish of $46\frac{1}{2}$lb. The film cameraman's patience was indeed well rewarded, for he got film of the entire battle.

To a great extent, the experienced salmon angler knows the signs and seasons when a certain method will bring him the best chance of sport, but if, like many salmon anglers, he has to book a beat in advance and perhaps travel several hundred miles, he will never know ideal conditions for the particular stretch of water he is to fish. If the early months are his chosen time, then it is a fairly safe bet that the spinning bait fished slow and deep will be the wisest choice. Alternatively, a classic beat in May could well see near-ideal conditions for the small fly on a floating line. But, even though fish may be caught, there will never be the certainty that sport was up to full potential.

From all this it could well be argued that the nomadic salmon angler, while experiencing a great variety of different rivers, will never have that intimate knowledge that would make him conscious of what, in my opinion, is of paramount importance to successful salmon fishing—the height of the water.

The angler who is fortunate enough not only to live on the banks of a salmon river but also to have access to the fishing, must have advantages far out-weighing any other considerations. By the continued fishing of one stretch of water over the years, he will know, perhaps quite unconsciously, when it is worth putting a line in the water and when it is more profitable to stay at home. The casual visitor has no such luck; he can only fish diligently during his chosen time in the hope of sport.

The reputed dourness of many Scottish gillies when they are dragged to the riverbank by enthusiastic tenants may well be the result of their knowledge that, could they themselves fish the river at that time, they would stay away. For this reason, the finest fisherman in the land would be hard put to compete with a local expert on his own stretch of water. The native would know the precise height when certain pools would fish best; he would also know the alternate lies on varying heights and the precise method most likely to achieve success.

For the non-resident angler, who consistently takes the beat of a river at the same season every year, the odds get narrowed down. He might very well spend the first two or three years serving an apprenticeship to the water, but if he persists he will begin to acquire some of the knowledge of the native and will ultimately be in a position to exploit every favourable condition. There will doubtless be occasions when he will find the river either dead low or in roaring flood, but he will at least be able to draw on his experience to know whether fishing is worthwhile or not, at any given height. While it might seem desirable to fish a great variety of rivers, the angler who persists with one particular beat will be able to fish with greater potential than the roving angler.

In his excellent little book *Rod fishing for salmon on the Wye*, J Arthur Hutton states quite categorically that the height of the water is, in his opinion, the most important factor in successful salmon fishing. I would endorse those remarks and would only add that I feel that temperature must also be closely linked with it, as must overhead conditions and humidity. With these points in their correct order, and fish in the pools, the choice of a particular fly or bait is comparatively elementary.

The late A H E Wood, who was perhaps the finest example of one-man-one-beat for season after season, when he fished the Cairnton beat of the Dee, said: 'As regards pattern, I do not believe this matters at all. Blue Charm and Silver Blue are my stock, simply on the principle that one is more or less black and the other white and so give me a choice. I once fished through a whole season with a March Brown only, and got my share, and more, of the fish caught.' This from a man whose annual salmon catch was in the region of 300 fish. Wood doubtless knew, by nothing more than a casual glance at the river, whether it was worthwhile fishing or not.

Again, Richard Waddington, when commenting on advanced techniques in greased-line fishing, said: 'Nor do I personally very much mind what pattern of fly I use . . . I have seen seasons when the Silver Blue was first choice—or a Logie or Jeannie. Today it appears to be the Hairy Mary. All these, and many other patterns, catch fish equally well, and it is only wishful thinking that invests any pattern with magic qualities.'

Wood was the typical example of an angler fortunate enough to live on his own stretch of water. Waddington, to my knowledge, did not actually live on a river but had sufficient access to a well-known beat of the Spey to know the water in all its moods and how best to take advantage of prevailing conditions.

Some of my earliest salmon fishing was done on the Argyllshire Awe. Yet I was to visit that river for three seasons before I caught my first Awe salmon. On future visits successes became more frequent and although I have not now fished the river for a number of years, I reckon I could still go back, at my chosen time, with great expectations of sport. Of late years I have tended to concentrate my salmon fishing on just two rivers, the Tweed and the Lune.

I take a beat on the Tweed for the same periods each year—two weeks in the early part of February and a further two weeks at the end of November—and I have now been visiting that river for ten years. I could not possibly claim to have the intimate knowledge of the beat that the local gillie has, but I do know it pretty intimately and from sheer experience I know its varying moods at differing heights of water and always get my share, and more, of the fish caught.

Over recent years I have had the good fortune to share a beat of the Lune with the well-known salmon angler, Reg Righyni, and although we are great friends we sometimes agree to differ on theories and certain aspects of technique. Righyni is an accomplished salmon angler, but as I also catch my share of the fish, the points upon which we differ are obviously only minor ones. We are pretty unanimous on basics. If, however, there was ever a stretch of water that is more influenced by its height, I have yet to see it.

Unfortunately, we do not have a measuring gauge on the river, but there is one small rock that, when it is just showing out of the water, tells me that the river is at near-perfect height. For me, it is as good as a micrometer for by reading it carefully I usually know whether I can expect the sport to be good or indifferent.

A typical occasion was when I was to visit the river for a period of three days with another well-known angler as my guest. We arrived at the river one Thursday evening in late July 1966. I had heard that the river was in fine trim with plenty of fish about, but on arrival I was greatly dismayed to learn that there had been further rain and my tell-tale rock was nowhere to be seen. My companion, who had fished the river on two previous occasions only, thought it looked perfect and quickly tackled up and was away before I had time to unload the car. For my own part I was in no hurry. We were to spend a few nights living rough-shod in the fishing hut and I spent the evening preparing the camp beds and generally tidying up the hut. When this was completed, I relaxed in a deck chair and, over a cosy glass of the wine of Scotland, I watched the sunset.

Darkness had fallen before my companion returned; he had seen several fish but had not touched one, nor had the sea-trout obliged in the failing light. Over a few more drams we discussed the prospects for the morning before turning into our sleeping bags for some quiet, peaceful sleep.

At six o'clock my companion was up and about, clambering into waders and generally disturbing the entire household! With one sleepy eye open I raised my head off the pillow to look out of the hut window to see what was happening to my rock. It was still not to be seen, although a faint wave line could now be detected from the water disturbance it was causing. I slumped back on to my pillow again and wished my companion the best of luck, tight lines and all that.

By ten o'clock he was back again, fishless, hungry and keen to get at the bacon and eggs I was frying over the cooker. This time he had seen even more fish and was completely mystified why at least one of them had not taken. Fully refreshed, he was soon back on the water, while I contented myself taking pictures. By nightfall on that Friday evening he was still fishless and was rapidly coming to the conclusion that the fish were uncatchable. Before I turned in, however, I had a last look at my rock and quietly observed that the slightest tip of it was now showing. With no more rain the river would be perfect for the morning.

At six o'clock the next morning it was I who was up and about creating a commotion and it was my friend who, between intermittent snores, risked one sleepy eye at me, with the news that he would have some breakfast ready by eight.

At eight o'clock I. was back—with three prime salmon, all covered in sea-lice and all in the 'teens of pounds. This was too much for him! What had I caught them on? 'A 2in black and gold,' I said. With that he was off, armed to the teeth with 2in black and golds, while I completed my breakfast. By ten o'clock my little rock was showing just a little more, so I put the spinning rod on one side and got my fly tackle ready. A No.6 Blue Charm seemed about right for the conditions and I waded across the river to join my friend, to find him still fishless. By mid-day I had two more fish on fly and it was not until one o'clock that my companion finally got one to take his spinner. By two o'clock we had to be on our way to join another friend on another river, but I left with mixed feelings, for I sensed that had I been able to fish that day out I should have broken the record for the beat.

Although paramount, the height of the water is not the only guide to a successful day. Other factors must combine to give the perfect day. And it is only by the intimate knowledge of one piece of water that these can be accurately judged.

December 1969   *Arthur Oglesby*

How temperature affects fishing

Although the fisherman cannot alter the temperature it is an advantage to know how it will affect his fishing, especially if he lives beside the water and is able to choose his day.

In early spring most of our rivers run cold with melting snow. If the river is much colder than the sea, salmon may not enter it, preferring to wait until it is warmer. Those salmon, however, that are bound for some tributary, which, draining lower land, is warmer than the main river, may swim through bitterly cold water in order to reach that sidestream, which, they seem to know instinctively, will be warmer.

A low temperature makes them torpid and they will ascend slowly by short stages. Cold water is therefore an advantage to the lower beats, as it holds the fish back at the expense of the higher beats. Conversely, if the water is warm, fish are likely to swim through the lower part of the river without pausing long enough to make the fishing in the lower pools productive.

Salmon do not play well in cold water. They are more likely to bore close at hand, making short, jerky runs. And if any fungus-infected fish come from the sea when the river is cold, the disease spreads rapidly, for it thrives in cold water, and heals only when the temperature rises or the infected fish return to salt water.

Ice may form on the bottom of the shallow streams, and when this breaks away, generally during the forenoon, it floats down as grue. When this happens it is almost impossible to fish as the grue runs down under the line and finally causes the fly or bait to tinkle over the top of the ice. If the line can be thrown along any lanes that are clear of grue and the rod point immediately submerged, some casts may be fished out.

For the first fortnight of February, fishing on the Tweed is limited to fly. If it happens to be cold, few fish will be caught, and it is only after the first day with a sprat that the fisherman gets some idea of the number of fish in the pools.

'The colder the water the larger the fly' is a good rule. Fish will not take the trouble to come to a small fly in cold water. They want to see something that looks worth while before bestirring themselves. The same rule applies to baits.

As the river gets warmer the salmon become more active. They play better when hooked and when fresh water comes they travel upstream further and faster. A reasonably warm river is therefore to be preferred and, as the water will still hold a good supply of oxygen, the fish are not likely to travel at all unless the river rises. If there is a succession of warm days, say late in May, the fish will probably travel even if the river is at summer level. This is because the water has got too warm and the fish generally begin to swim at the warmest time of the day, say about two o'clock in the afternoon, hoping to find a higher oxygen content further up. This, of course, unsettles them. Salmon indeed take best in a medium temperature.

The big autumn salmon are not likely to settle and take well unless there is some night frost. Some fishermen think that frost wakens them up and so makes them take. That is a fallacy: the frost does just the opposite. If there is no frost to chill the water and even if the river is steady, the autumn fish may continue to travel sufficiently to keep them unsettled, so that they will not take well. The frost, by cooling the river, stops them from travelling, unless there is extra water, and so makes them better takers.

Fishing with a fly in autumn when it is actually freezing is as unproductive as it is in early spring. Normally the last of the light or before or after the red sunset, if there is one, is a good time to catch autumn fish. If, however, one feels that tingle on the fingers, which indicates frost, there is no point in continuing to fish, even though there is no immediate change in the general water temperature. Fish swim nearer to the bottom in cold water—or if the air is cold—and the moment frost comes on they drop down.

Because cold makes salmon swim deeper than they would in warmer conditions, greased-line is unproductive if the water is colder than say 48°F. Greased-line is a summer method, when the air is seldom if ever cold enough to make the fish swim near the bottom. The air temperature in summer is not therefore of great importance as it is not often more than a few degrees different from that of the water. As long, therefore, as the water is not below say 48°F this method should be successful. It is possible to have a big day, with water say 52°F and air say 48°F, although it is generally, but not always, preferable to have the variation the other way round. If, for example, the water was as hot as say 63°F then an air temperature of 60°F would give better results than one of say 70°F. If the water is warmer than say 65°F, and the air temperature higher still, the prospects are poor, as there is a lack of oxygen. It is only when salmon are swimming close to the surface that they will trouble to come to the small flies that are used on a greased-line in the summer.

Keeping these remarks about air temperature in mind, we have a complication caused by a cold wind actually hitting the water. The general air temperature is not sufficiently low to affect the fishing, and fish will take where the cold wind is not striking the surface. The fish will not, however, take where this wind does hit the water and this is especially true if the wind has come on suddenly. Such a wind will stop the fish taking a bait as well as a fly, be the latter fished on sunk- or greased-line. The reason for this is, I think, that the cold wind cools the surface of the water. This cold wind will cool the surface film almost immediately. Whenever this happens a thin layer of cold water descends as it is replaced by warmer water from underneath. Therefore, as long as that wind hits the water the surface film is constantly being cooled, so that cold water is continually dropping down on to the fish. This presumably is as uncomfortable to them as a draught of cold air is to us, and so stops them from taking. The water in a loch would, of course, behave in the same way as it does in a river, and that is the probable reason why a cold wind stops fish from taking wherever it hits the surface—but only where it does actually hit the water.

In conclusion, temperatures of air and water that are normal for the time of year are preferable, and extremes spoil the chances, just as too much or too little water, or immoderate wind or sunshine will limit the bag.

May 1957   *G P R Balfour-Kinnear*

What does a salmon see?

A salmon's eyes, we are told, can neither focus accurately nor distinguish detail; they cannot be shut, so are dazzled by strong light; and they are probably colour blind. But they are sensitive to movement, can perceive tone, if not colour, and are quite efficient in a poor light. Each eye can cover almost the whole field on its own side, but the two can see together only within a small angle straight in front of the fish. No wonder a concoction of fur and feather is occasionally mistaken for something else!

It is obvious that a salmon's eyes are not like ours, so we can never really know what it actually sees. Even if some earnest seeker after knowledge, with all the right equipment, were to lie down on the bottom of a pool, he would be able to tell us only what he himself saw, and we can form a pretty good idea of that without putting anyone to so much trouble, for we do know something about the physical properties of light and water, and how reflection and refraction affect our own vision; and they must also affect what the fish sees, even though what it sees may not appear the same to it as it does to us.

There is nothing in what is known about a salmon's eyes to prevent it seeing even a small fly if it is moving, provided the light is not too strong and the water is clear, fairly still and free from obstructions—and we know that, in fact, it does.

A fish will come from some distance away to take a fly in these conditions if it is attracted by it. But the water is not always clear, still and unobstructed—far from it. In lochs, except for a ruffled surface, it is often so; in rivers, seldom.

The water in a river is nearly always in motion and to some extent turbulent. The turbulence may be slight in a big, deep pool with little current, or where the bottom is smooth; but where the bed of a river contains many rocks or boulders, or if the current is fast—often the two go together—it is usually considerable.

Turbulent water affects vision in two ways: anything seen through it appears blurred or distorted, and the surface, being uneven, can neither be seen through clearly nor act as a true mirror. In still water, as we well know, vision through the surface from below is confined to a circle, a little over 40 degrees from the vertical in all directions around the point of view. This is the 'window' of the fish. Outside it, all that can be seen is beneath the surface and may either be seen directly or as a reflection from its underside, sometimes both.

But this is only if the surface is even. If, because of waves or turbulence, it is moving or uneven, what is seen from below it must appear quite different: vision through it now becomes only partial, interrupted by dancing reflections, and the mirror outside the 'window' is no longer true—it moves, the image is blurred and fleeting views of the world above the river appear through it.

I should perhaps apologise for repeating all this, which must be so well known to many fishers for salmon; but it seems worth reminding ourselves that it is only in water that is fairly still, as well as being clear, that a fish is likely to be able to see far, or at all distinctly—and even then, only when it is not dazzled by too strong a light.

We know only too well what a bright sun shining down a pool does to our fishing prospects! And the reason, of course, is not (as is sometimes alleged) that the fish then sees too much, but that it can hardly see at all. Sun from one side of the river or the other is less harmful, because one eye of the fish is probably less dazzled by it.

So a slow, deep pool with few big boulders in it, on a day of low cloud, no doubt affords a fish as good and as long a view as, in a river, it is ever likely to get. If a large, well-sunk fly (or a spun bait if you like) is cast into it, it will probably be seen by the fish before it comes anywhere near it. But a small fly near the surface is likely to be seen from much further away; for not only will the fish see two flies--the real one and its image reflected from the surface—but it will see both of them better than a larger fly lower down in the water. And the two may well look different since the real one, seen from below, will appear dark, while the image, lit from above, will appear lighter and brighter.

While, therefore, it seems perfectly reasonable to fish a sunk fly down such a pool with fairly short intervals between casts (apart from anything else, we do this when the water is cold and the fish disinclined to move far to take), is it equally sensible to adopt the same tactics with a fly that is only just submerged? The sight of a pair of similar, if not quite identical, objects slowly advancing in a succession of sweeps across the pool must begin to pall after a bit! And by the time one of them (and perhaps the more attractive of the

two) disappears in the 'window' above the fish, it has probably
already decided against taking it, for if it were attracted by it, it
would surely have at least moved towards it soon after it first saw it.

At the opposite extremes, however, a fish lying in broken, rapid
water is unlikely to see any object in it clearly until it is quite close to
it. A fly low in the water will be obscured by boulders and distorted
by turbulence: one near the surface will be even more distorted, its
reflection intermittent, its background a mere jumble of sky and
bottom, and not until it gets into the 'window' will it appear at all
distinctly. It is in places like this, where the fish has difficulty in
seeing the fly clearly, that one tries to present it in such a manner as
to give it the best possible chance of doing so.

This does not mean casting repeatedly in the same place, which is
seldom profitable, but trying various presentations in the hope that
one of them may be successful.

In between these two extremes of good and bad visibility, there
are innumerable lies in all sorts of places, from which the fish can see
with varying degrees of clearness. It pays, I am sure, to study each
one from the point of view of the fish and what one imagines it can
see, and then, and only then, to try to place one's fly accordingly. In
some pools, relatively few casts may be enough to ensure that every
fish had had a good view of the fly. In others—perhaps smaller
ones—more, and more varied kinds of cast, will be needed to
achieve the same end. Unimaginative casting is seldom rewarding.

It is much to be deplored, but the more one considers this question
of visibility from beneath the surface of a river, the more one comes
to the conclusion that the best colour for a fly fished high in the water
is black! And this is irrespective of whether the fish is colour-blind or
not, since in most places a fly of any colour must appear dark
against the surface: it is only when its reflection is clearly seen that
any variation in tone or colour can appear.

The slow, even-flowing pool with a still surface may be an
exception. And we may perhaps make one small concession—a
flash of light may help to attract attention; so a streak of white in the
fly, or a silver hook or treble, may well have its uses. But generally
speaking a black fly of the right shape and size is all that is needed.
This is a most depressing conclusion for those of us who enjoy trying
different flies when our favourite one is unsuccessful—but is it not
borne out by our experiences?

It is not at all the same, of course, with a fly that is fished deep, because it is seen not against the surface, but against the general background of the pool. Any colour it may have will therefore be as clear to the fish as it ever can be, and if it is tone rather than colour that the fish perceives, there is still plenty of scope for a fly that is not black.

So far, I have been assuming that the water is clear. If there is colour in the river, there may also be some point in using a coloured fly, even if it is fished near the surface. I have myself found that a March Brown or a Lady Caroline can be successful when a spate is clearing enough for a fly to be visible at all; and others have found an Ackroyd to be good then. I think this is because in these conditions, which we always associate with good fishing prospects, the surface plays a less important part than it does when the water is clear. The important thing is that the fly should be easily visible through the coloured water; and since it is often more or less brown, a fly of similar tone will be most clearly seen. Peat-stained water is usually bad for fishing because of its acidity; so it is hardly surprising that a suitable fly for it is not easy to discover.

It is as well to remember, incidentally, that visibility from below, upwards, in coloured water is much better than visibility from above, downwards; so a river clearing after a spate often becomes fishable sooner than we might expect. And because the light is diffused and reflections likely to be dim, a surface-fished fly may be seen against a more uniform and less confusing background, and so perhaps, paradoxically, it may be better defined. But this is venturing rather far into the realms of speculation.

March 1973   *Robin Elles*

The unconventional hours

Salmon fishermen tend to observe rather conventional hours such as 'on the water about ten' and 'back in time for a bath before dinner'. During the spring and early summer this time-table effectively covers the best taking periods. Indeed, one will be unlikely to catch many fish outside these hours.

But in the summer when the water is low, skies are bright and the salmon are becoming stale it is a different matter. Other tactics are called for then and the first step is, I believe, to reverse one's normal fishing hours. Prospects from ten till six will be poor, unless one is lucky enough to be blessed with a convenient spate. Instead, the times when the salmon will be likeliest to show an interest in a fly will be the evening, the early morning and even during the night.

There is undoubtedly an 'evening rise' for salmon as for trout. It starts as the light begins to fade and may continue for an hour or more after sunset, always provided that mist does not come down on the water. The first hour after the sun has disappeared can be one of the best, especially for the larger fish. I may be prejudiced in favour of that hour, having caught my largest-ever salmon in the dusk and on the last of my 'five last casts'! On Canada's east coast this after-sunset fishing is well known and is even referred to as 'the fool's half-hour'. It is also well known to many gillies on this side of the Atlantic and may explain that casual parting remark: 'I thought I might just have a cast or two while you're at dinner, sir, if I may.'

Salmon seem to become restless and more active as the light fades in the evening and they are more interested in taking. They no longer sulk in sullen indifference on the river bottom but tend to move their lies. Some may drop down the pool into calmer water while others will move up further into the run. It pays, therefore, to fish the whole length of the pool, rather than just the well-known daytime spots. There is no need, I have found, to change to a larger fly, but it does pay to fish it fairly slowly.

Although the real 'evening rise' for salmon seems to last only for the hour or so immediately after sunset while there is still a glimmer of light in the sky, salmon may also take in complete darkness, in the same way as sea-trout. It is possible on some rivers to catch them throughout the night, as was clearly proved by one Scottish landowner recently. He had been suffering badly from poachers, who were regularly and ruthlessly raiding his best pools. They did their dirty work by night. He therefore arranged with several of his friends and neighbours that they would fish his water every night and all night on a roster. The plot worked perfectly in that the poachers were effectively thwarted. It also had a further and perhaps slightly surprising success, because the legitimate anglers managed to catch several salmon almost every night.

Night fishing for salmon can be effective under suitable conditions but it is, I believe, more profitable and also rather more pleasant to try one's luck early in the morning. The fishing can be excellent and it is a wonderful time to be at the water's edge. There is also the advantage that the fish have not been disturbed unduly during the night. The best time is the hour or so immediately after sunrise, though the taking period may well last up to three or four hours. And what could be more satisfying than to return to breakfast with a salmon already to one's credit for the day?

I know one highly skilled fisherman who customarily drives his guests over forty miles to fish his river as soon after dawn as he can manage to get them there. He expects that at least one fish will be taken in the first few hours of the day and his personal best is five before breakfast. He then usually leaves the fishing during the day to the more conventionally-minded syndicate on the other bank.

With our limited knowledge of the psychology of salmon it is still a matter of speculation as to why a salmon should take at one time of the day rather than another. But there are several possible reasons why the evening and early morning should be particularly good during the summer. First, fish are understandably shy in conditions of bright sunlight and low water. They naturally feel safer in the dark and tend to take best in the twilight when they still have some light but not enough to make them feel vulnerable. Then there is also the question of whether fish ever sleep, and if so, when. One experienced angler is convinced that, anyway during the summer, salmon take a siesta regularly during the heat of the day and 'wake up' again later in the day.

The late A H E Wood at Cairnton on the Aberdeenshire Dee evidently had some confidence in this theory. His guests used to be invited, on occasion, to relax between a late lunch and 'high tea' at about six o'clock. They were then sent out to fish until dark and sometimes even until midnight.

Another factor is undoubtedly the temperature and oxygen content of the water. One cannot generalise on this, as it varies from river to river, but it must be fair to say that the condition of almost any water will not be the same at night as during a hot summer's day, and that this change will be noticeable to the fish. If this is so they would, like human beings, naturally have different habits for night and day, and would be particularly active and alert in the transitory periods at dusk and dawn.

It follows from this that it should pay to concentrate one's fishing effort during the summer months on the twilight hours and, if you feel like it, on the night time as well.

May 1965   *Julian Paget*

Making hay—on Wye!

Speaking lightly about the River Wye is as reprehensible as making wisecracks about the Test or mentioning that the Itchen has some good eel fishing. Unfortunately, my relationship with the Wye has always had flippant undertones. They date back to the first time I fished there twenty-one years ago, and even now, after a week on it, in 1971, if pressed, I find it hard to resist calling it a splendid coarse-fishing river.

If fishermen worship one thing, it is expertise. They follow slavishly the laws and writings of the pundits, taking water temperatures, changing from floating to sunk lines at the drop of a degree and tracing complex patterns across the fishes' lies. Salmon fishing is no longer the simple exercise it was before UDN and Greenland. That is why I feel embarrassed at revealing, for the first time, my simpleton behaviour on that maiden salmon fishing holiday.

'Our guests may fish,' the hotel brochure crooned, 'in one of the Wye's most famous salmon pools.' I packed my wife and a borrowed 16ft fly-rod into the car and set off for Herefordshire.

There was a heatwave at the time—something that I now realise is normal in the Wye valley. The river was low and clear, running between banks of weed, not unlike, it seemed to me, the upper reaches of the Thames. Where it was markedly different was in the sight and sound of enormous red, 'potted' salmon, leaping lethargically from their lies like small porpoises.

I had been by one of the river's most famous pools for only a matter of minutes when a huge fish boiled opposite me, at the other side of a massive weed-bank. The 16ft rod waved and a large bushy Jock Scott was delivered into the water 3ft upstream of the dying ripples. As it floated down there was a splash and a boil and the rod bent like a reed.

'Got one,' I shouted to my wife, who to her everlasting credit ran straight into the river, fully clothed, brandishing a gaff. Neither of us knew what was going to happen. Neither of us was prepared for the 3lb fish that, under immense pressure, popped from the weed-bank like a cork from a bottle. I had caught my first Wye chub.

Four years later and much, much wiser, I took three days' holiday to recover from an unnecessarily vicious attack of tonsilitis. I went to another Wye-side hotel, which advertised a mile-and-a-half of fishing. The temperatures were in the high seventies, but just previously there had been heavy rain. The river was mountainous and mud brown. Even if the hotel fishing had been good, it was going to be days before conditions were favourable.

Our best pool was fished from the top of a toll-bridge, and I wondered, as I cast lethargically into the torrent below, what would happen if a fish took my spinner. None did. The only fish I heard of was taken on a bunch of worms from the small lawn at the rear of some tea-gardens, on which the two enterprising ladies who made the dainty teas sold fishing tickets for 25p a day. We did not catch one there, either.

My attitude to the Wye was not helped by the experience of a doctor friend who had never before fished in the Wye or in any other river, and who was invited by a patient to fish his beat when passing close to Hereford on his way home from Ireland. He was handed a rod to which a massive Yellow Belly was attached. He hurled the lure towards the other bank, hooked and landed a sixteen-pounder, put it in the back of his car and continued his journey. He telephoned me that night to tell me about it. 'What sort of fish was it,' I asked him, meaning was it fresh-run or red. 'It was a . . .,' he paused, 'salmon, I think it was.' For some reason I have always told this story as a joke against the Wye.

This year, by a stroke of good fortune (and the benevolence of Mr Dare at the Crown Hotel, Hay-on-Wye), I had the opportunity of fishing a beat two miles upstream of Hay Bridge, an experience that upset most of my preconceived ideas of Wye fishing. It was a superb piece of fly fishing (and spinning, too, for that matter) with two long, fast runs culminating in holding pools and an even longer flat with sufficient current at the far side to work a fly, ending with a pool that covered several acres and that was fished, if at all, from a boat.

The river in the runs ran fast and clear over rocks and smooth stones, and from our bank we fished from wadeable shallows to deep lies. I should perhaps add that I no longer wave bushy Jock Scotts at jumping salmon.

The normal Wye heatwave was in full swing and the river, unfortunately, was several inches too low and dropping lower each day. Nevertheless, I persevered with hope, taking water and air temperatures with determination and a wink, alternatively using sinking and floating lines, and experimenting with flies of all sizes.

I was well into my second day before I had my first pull. It came only seconds before instant hopes of a salmon were turned into a less optimistic surmise of a decent trout; then the inevitable realisation that a trout would have behaved more savagely. It turned out to be a 2lb chub with a nice friendly face.

By the end of my stay of four days my score was: salmon, nil; friendly chub, three; and a perch of $2\frac{1}{2}$lb (my biggest ever)—all caught on salmon flies, over salmon lies. But for one thing I would be tempted to make remarks about splendid, if expensive, coarse fishing.

On the day I left, I went to the fishing hut to collect my tackle and then on to the river to say goodbye to the amiable opposition. He was standing, pale-faced, by the chub pool having just lost a fish, estimated at 30lb, which had gobbled his fly and after twenty minutes made off with it and 2yd of 15lb nylon. From this moment on I can only look with reverence and awe at a river in which this kind of adventure takes place in a heatwave and after an eight-week drought. In fact, I'm hoping to return to the same place next year.

August 1971   *David Barr*

Salmon on the fast fly

Many years ago on the Ross-shire Blackwater, anglers used to 'dibble' their flies in the white water, causing a wake, and they caught salmon. Although the fly was stationary, relative to the current it was travelling fast.

The idea occurred to me, years later, that salmon would take a fast-moving fly, certainly in slacker water and even in the stream. At first I merely mended downstream instead of up and caught fish. Then a season or so later I found myself not only mending down to speed up the fly, but recovering line by hand as well.

I continued to catch fish and by this time was catching salmon when, during periods of inactivity, others, myself included, were not getting them by the normal method. On rivers such as the Ewe, where there was a population of large sea-trout as well as salmon, both species were attracted to the fast-moving fly and, in fact, I caught sea-trout in the daytime when the normal method usually failed.

Then I was introduced to the General Practitioner fly, with its long tail extending back to more than twice the length of its hook. I wondered how to fish this fly when I was given it to try out and, as with all new flies, I tried when fish had not been taking anything for some time, on the Boat Pool of the Conon—an unfair thing to do with a new pattern, perhaps.

The Boat Pool is a big place with a rippleless current and really needs wind as well as a flow. However, I put on the GP and cast it as far as I could straight across the pool. Then I recovered the fly in a series of jerks, believing that it looked well swimming like a shrimp or prawn. Apparently, the fish thought so too and they came for it. I caught a number of fish that week on the GP worked fast when no one else (or I) could catch them on flies fished in an orthodox manner.

Since then I have speeded up the recovery when using this fly and my technique now is to cast square and really get the fly coming back at me in swift jerks, each one 4–5ft long. At the same time as I gather in a yard or more of line, I lift the rod point high, then pause, drop the rod and repeat the process until the fly is at my bank.

The perspicacious reader will realise that a by no means small problem has occurred if a fish has taken the fly with yards and yards of line at one's feet. This line has to be got rid of without it being wrapped round feet, buttons and so on.

In a pool such as I have described, one can see fish start out to chase the fly and the distance they travel for it is quite astonishing. I have seen a fish start a bow wave 12yd away. Sometimes they boil at the fly more than once as it progresses across the pool, but when they take it they do so very thoroughly indeed and are nearly always well hooked.

I believe that salmon will chase any long-tailed fly like the GP because I have used other patterns successfully, such as the Garry Dog, which is suitable with its long yellow hair extending well beyond the hooks.

A number of fish will chase the fly across the pool and not finally take it. When this happens I have never had them come a second time. So, consequently, I make only one cast from a given stance and, because they appear to see it for 12yd or so, I move downstream about 3yd between each cast. Therefore, I fish a pool quickly and I am sure by doing so the pool is not disturbed. I know this to be so because I and my friends have taken fish the next time down.

It is rather an exhausting way to fish and I use this method only when fish are dour and not taking. Some of my medical friends say it is a good 'diagnostic aid' because often it seemed to make fish visibly come at the fly when otherwise they were not showing and, therefore, not known to be in the pool.

But at other times I work the small fly, although not so briskly as the GP, quite quickly through the water and a substantial proportion of my fish caught in the summer are taken by a quickly moving fly.

Even in the spring, when one's thoughts are of a large and heavy fly sinking deep and moving slowly through the pool, I tend to get it moving faster than most people. I do this by hand-lining and I believe that an eager springer will travel further than is generally realised to take the fly. Anyhow, I have had good results by employing this method on the Shin and Blackwater. My choice of fly in the spring for this kind of fishing is a Beaulieu Snow Fly tied on a $2\frac{1}{2}$–3in tube, with lots of long loose peacock herl to give much movement as I recover it. A Garry Dog of the same length and dressed in the same way, with a generous helping of loose yellow and red hair, is also successful.

Having described my method of fishing the salmon fly quickly, I would add that my own successes in angling are not entirely attributable to this method. I believe that one can get the maximum number of fish from a salmon beat if one is prepared to ring the changes. Speed of fly relative to the current, size and colour, all have their part to play, of course, but he who is prepared to experiment has a better chance than the more conservative angler.

I well remember the day when a well-known personality on the Beauly, who was to fish down the pool behind me, said: 'How did you fish the pool? In the usual way?' I replied: 'I did. I mended up.' He promptly fished the pool out by mending downstream so that his fly came into the vision of the fish quite differently from mine and although I cannot say he caught a fish on that occasion, the lesson was there to be learnt.

January 1970   *William Brown*

Fish that come unstuck

Is there not more to be learned from fish lost than from fish caught? And how much duller would fishing be if fish never were lost!

The causes of losses, both avoidable and unavoidable, are legion—the unavoidable being certainly less interesting—and it is the object of this article to investigate and comment.

Of the unavoidable losses, the hook coming away is the most common, and a skin or light gristle hold (which is nobody's fault) makes this almost inevitable sooner or later during play. Incidentally, if the angler suspects a fish to be lightly hooked, he does well to keep downstream of it as much as possible, pulling the hook back into its mouth; and it is possible that he may succeed in landing it by holding it lightly, especially in the closing stages.

Intermittent bad patches in nylon monofilament are a common cause of breaks, though much less frequent nowadays with the improved nylon. If there is any uncertainty, however, the whole reel of nylon should be ruthlessly scrapped. Hooks also can break without warning, especially when of fine wire and when a fish has been played for a long time. Modern tempering leaves something to be desired.

With light tackle in a strong river, it may be almost impossible to avoid a loss through a sizeable fish running out a long line and 'drowning' it; equally, it may be impossible in spite of all efforts to keep a fish away from snags. The moral is don't fish too light!

If a dropper is being used, when a fish has been hooked, there is always the chance of the disengaged fly fouling an obstruction, in spite of all precautions, or of a second fish taking it or being fouled by it. In either case, a break is likely, so that using a dropper involves a calculated risk.

One other and unusual way in which a fish can become unhooked occurs when a double- or treble-hooked fly is used, and when during the play the antics of the fish cause the nylon to get wedged backwards between the bends of the hooks, thus virtually acting as a hook extractor!

Losses such as these would seem unavoidable, even if all reasonable precautions are taken. But of greater interest are the many types of avoidable losses that teach useful lessons! The most frequent causes of these are badly tied knots that slip, bad gaffing, hook points broken or blunted on stones behind, rotten or jammed backing that was not previously tested, or that was even parting from the main line through bad splicing. All these can be said to be fairly common, with obvious remedies.

Another frequent cause of breaks, perhaps more frequent than suspected, is wind knots formed in the nylon during casting. Such knots must be eliminated as soon as formed, since an ordinary overhand knot lessens the breaking-strain of nylon by about 65 per cent. They are apt to creep in unnoticed, particularly on windy days, and most of the 'inexplicable' breaks in nylon are caused by them.

And how many fish are lost every year through the reel falling off during the excitement of play? Plenty, no doubt, and how can the fisherman be excused for this?

To have a hooked fish break you on known snags is more uncertain, and sometimes with a strong and wild fish the fisherman must have the benefit of the doubt; but at other times it can be patently his fault through lack of control.

Using too light tackle when there are big fish about is also a calculated risk that may well end in disaster, especially on big rivers such as the Spey or Tay. And don't use small hooks where the fish run big, or vice versa; both lead to preventable losses.

'Drowned' lines can often cause losses, especially in sizeable rivers. But experienced anglers can often avoid getting their line drowned by holding the rod high or by moving quickly on to a high bank and making every effort to keep as much line out of the water as possible.

Holding a fish too hard when playing is another fault, particularly in the case of small salmon and grilse, which have tender mouths. On the other hand, the longer a hooked fish is in the water, the greater chance of losing him. So try to strike the happy mean in the amount of pressure used in playing. 'When he pulls, let him run. When he stops pulling, you pull him back!' This is normally sound advice.

Don't reel a fish in too close during the early stages of play. Sometimes a fish will come in tamely and on to a short line while still full of vigour. If he then suddenly thrashes and/or jumps, you will probably lose him. It is safer to walk away from him and keep him on a reasonable length of line. And, needless to say, never commit the elementary fault of reeling the knot between line and cast through the top rod-ring! It will almost certainly jam.

Landing-nets sometimes give trouble. Watch out for holes and rotten meshes. And don't let a fish run into the outside of the net when almost played out. An exposed hook-point will then lead to almost certain loss.

When beaching a fish, don't attempt to pull him up too steep a slope. He may break or become unhooked. Find an easier beach, or just steady him and tail him. Also, when he is on the bank, make sure that he has been fairly knocked on the head and is dead! He might jump back into the river; it has happened before now!

Abuse of hooks is another frequent cause of loss. Perhaps the point has been blunted or broken on stones in casting. Carborundum stone is useful for sharpening them. And bent hooks should be scrapped; to bend them back into shape and continue using them, is asking for a break in weakened metal next time a fish is hooked.

Finally, one cause of failure to hook fish can be through a double- or treble-hooked fly being fished upside down because the nylon is jammed between the bend of the hooks. In this case, a good pull from a fish is the best that can be expected! Most fishermen have experienced this and it is apt to happen often, so watch out for it!

Other more abstruse causes of loss and their remedies can be left to readers' imaginations. Regrettably, carelessness on the part of the fisherman is the normal root of the trouble. The avoidance of such carelessness, with meticulous attention to detail, forms a large part of the fascination of fishing.

June 1973   *John Ashley-Cooper*

Where have all the big ones gone?

Quite often one hears and reads anglers bemoaning the decline in big salmon, the forty- and fifty-pounders. And not only anglers. Only a few months ago that well-known authority, Dr Arthur Went of the Irish Department of Agriculture and Fisheries wrote: 'In recent years large salmon (over 25lb in weight) have been comparatively scarce in Irish waters, as they have been in some other countries'—for which read 'the whole of the British Isles'.

Anglers usually attribute this decline of the 'portmanteau' (forty-pounders) and the 'American travelling trunk' (fifty-pounder) to various malevolent agencies—estuary nets, sea nets, disease and from time to time to various other sources well-known to be conspiring against the well-being of the salmon angler.

In fact, their temporary absence is certainly largely, and probably entirely, due to certain aspects of the changing patterns of the runs, which I would now like to discuss. Readers may note my optimistic use of the word 'temporary'. There are ample signs over the last ten years or so that the numbers of heavy salmon are slowly on the increase again, particularly in the Tay and Tweed, but these are autumn fish, whereas from the 1910s until the 1950s most British rod-caught forty- and fifty-pounders were spring fish.

The great period for heavy salmon in British rivers was from the late nineteenth century to the 1940s. Their numbers were relatively small for most of the nineteenth century until towards its close, and slowly declined from the 1940s until very recent years. There is no accident whatever about this, but the great period was the result of two completely different trends, at once both contradictory and complementary.

During the earlier part of this period the summer runs of salmon ran later in many rivers, with much-increased average weights, and during the later part the spring runs increased and certain rivers became renowned for their early-running 'whoppers'. There was, of course, considerable overlapping of these trends in certain rivers, particularly the Tay. Let us examine a number of rivers with a view to validating the foregoing general theory.

It is not, perhaps, widely known that throughout the major part of the nineteenth century the main runs of salmon (and, of course, of grilse) in Britain were in the summer. As most salmon anglers think in terms of spring and autumn, I stress, the summer. The main exceptions to this rule were a small group of rivers on the north-eastern and northern coasts of Scotland noted for spring fish, and generally, smaller streams where the main run continued into the autumn.

In his *Angler's Companion*, written in the 1850s, Thomas Tod Stoddart said that the heaviest recorded rod-caught salmon 'of late years' was a fish of 36lb taken in 1849—surely a commonplace weight for the heaviest salmon in all Britain over a considerable number of years. Stoddart also recorded what he considered to be a net-caught fish of outstanding size—43½lb. Compare this with a section of a letter written about the Tay by P D Malloch in 1902: 'We have got two salmon in the nets over 60lb last week, and one yesterday 50lb.' Subsequently, the editor of *Angler's Companion*, Sir Herbert Maxwell, writing just after the turn of the century, felt constrained to comment: 'The maximum weight of salmon in both Tay and Tweed appears to have risen considerably since Stoddart's day, probably owing to the protection of kelts. Few seasons pass over the Tweed, and none over the Tay, without fish of over 40lb falling to the rod.' I am interested in Sir Herbert's proposition about kelts and believe there is an element of truth in it, but it does not account for the decline of heavy autumn fish since the early 1900s.

Throughout the greater part of the nineteenth century the salmon run in the Tweed peaked in July (grilse in August), and the average weight was low. In *Days and Nights of Salmon Fishing in the River Tweed*, written in the 1840s, Scrope said: 'During my experience of twenty years I never caught one there above thirty pounds, and very few above twenty.' And remember Scrope spent the whole of the summer and autumn fishing whenever the water was suitable, with both rod and spear. Compare this with a great day among other great days of Mr George M'Culloch at Lower Floors in 1903, when on 20 November, he took nineteen fish of an average weight of more than 20lb including no fewer than ten fish of 20lb or more, the biggest one of 39lb. Inspector of Salmon Fisheries Calderwood recorded the movement of the biggest net catches in the Tweed progressively from July to August, and then to September as the century drew near its end. This was reflected by the extension of the rod-closing date from 8 November to 30 November.

It was more or less exactly the same in the Tay in the late nineteenth and early part of this century. Malloch (manager of the Tay Salmon Fisheries Company) observed in his *Life History and Habits of the Salmon* (1909): 'I have noticed in our fish-house as many as forty fish over 40lb weight, all caught in one day with the nets.' In case readers think this is a misprint, I repeat: forty fish of more than 40lb weight in one day.

Although Malloch does not say so, these great catches were certainly all from the late run before the nets came off. He records the weights of the heaviest rod-caught fish from the Tay up to 1907. Of nine fish between 51 and 63lb none was caught earlier than 1870, and seven of them were caught in October between 1883 and 1907.

The later running of the summer fish towards the end of the nineteenth century was, of course, recorded in numerous other rivers, from the Thurso in Caithness, to the Taw in Devon. Sir Herbert Maxwell, in his own book *Salmon and Sea Trout* (1898) said of the Thurso that '. . . the autumn fishing, formerly of little value, is now excellent'. Of the Aberdeenshire Dee he observed: '. . . not only has the autumn angling greatly improved, but the average weight shows a marked increase.' And so on.

So much for the heavy autumn fish of the late nineteenth and early twentieth centuries. The gradual movement to spring-running patterns was taking place by stages at the same time and the great period of heavy spring fish both overlapped and followed the period for heavy autumn fish. Some rivers, for example the Tweed and

Aberdeenshire Dee, experienced a movement of the large grilse runs into runs of small two-sea-winter springers, and big spring fish were a great rarity—almost non-existent. In other rivers of great size, or fertility—i.e. many one-year smolts—three-sea-winter spring fish ran in large numbers throughout the spring cycle, and it was with this run that was associated the four- and even five-sea-winter leviathan class of spring fish. Nearly all this class, by the way, were maiden, as opposed to the heavy autumn fish which included a greater proportion of previous spawners.

In this class of river, the Wye, although it has competitors for pre-eminence, was perhaps without peer. For one thing, its big springers were consistently bigger than elsewhere; for another, it is convenient to use as a comparison because of the smallness of its fish in the nineteenth century and their typically summer-running habits: 'Very few fish were killed in March and April in old days, and the great bulk of the fish were then killed in June and July, even August, and this is corroborated by the late day on which fishing began in past times, namely 12 March.' (Gilbert.) The freshwater nettings tell the story of the weights: from 1870 to 1875, 1,553 fish were netted at Fownhope, average weight 9lb; 289 fish were netted at Courtfield in 1874, average weight 10lb.

The first Wye 50lb springer was killed in 1914 and from then through to the 1940s there was a steady stream of fifty- and sixty-pounders and numerous forty- to fifty-pounders. During this period the famous Robert Pashley killed no fewer than twenty-nine salmon of 40lb or more in the Wye—a record unparalleled in the British Isles. Very big spring fish have now declined in the Wye as elsewhere, though the river still almost invariably yields one or more forty-pounders each year, and a number of thirty- to forty-pounders. However, it is to the increasing autumn runs that we must in the future look for our forty- and fifty-pounders, and particularly in Tay and Tweed.

I have never caught a forty-pounder. One day in spring I was in a boat on the Tay when we caught only one clean fish. It weighed 43lb. Unfortunately, it was not my call on the 'poker'! In recent years on the Tay in the autumn my friend and fishing companion, Tom Briggs, caught one weighing 47lb and lost another whopper after one and a half hours, the line getting round his thumb and nearly removing it. It is indicative that Tom usually spins, while I usually

fish fly. These big autumn fellows don't seem to like greased-line flies.
We follow each other down the same big pools, and his average
weight is always higher than mine but mine are usually newer fish.

July 1976   *Tony George*

The good and the bad in spinning

I am always slightly jolted by the attitude some anglers have to
salmon spinning in Scotland. They regard it as a poor substitute for
fly fishing, to the extent that one sometimes feels that a salmon
brought into the hotel after a hard day's fishing is somehow devalued
because it was tempted by a brown and gold devon rather than a
No.6 Hairy Mary. Now I like fly fishing and wherever possible
would go out of my way to cover a salmon with fly rather than with
bait. But I do not accept the view that all spinning is mindless. Quite
the reverse. I believe spinning has a whole range of subtleties that the
average angler may well not know about. I am sure it is bad spinning
that gives rise to the slightly reproachful 'Oh' one hears when it is
revealed that one's fish took a bait.

I restrict my spinning to fishing on the larger rivers, and my usual
haunts are the Spey and Tay. Both can be good fly waters with
precedence established by the Spey. There, in varied streamy
conditions, a good fly fisher can wade and cover some productive
shallowish water that is ideally suited to the fly—especially the fly
fished on the floating line.

On the Tay, where there are larger pools and less productive
streamy fishing, fly is slightly more restricted, but not nearly as
restricted as some anglers seem to believe. Just to cheer them up, let
me say that from August onwards the Tay will yield as many, if not
more, salmon to a well-fished small fly than to devons, particularly
when the water is low. Even in early spring bait is not inevitable. I
have had two experiences of the first salmon of the season in
January coming to fly rather than to bait. Thus the argument one
hears so often on the Tay that fly fishing is useless is misleading. In

my opinion it covers up as an excuse for a great deal of mindless grinding of spinning reels and ever more mindless harling.

I have sometimes argued that good spinning is related to good fly fishing, but I may well have got the emphasis wrong. Good fly fishing and good spinning are both parts of good fishing, and that covers the intelligent use of the rod and the bait, the interpretation of the lie being fished and the handling of hooked fish. In fly fishing it is usually painfully obvious when someone can't cast; in spinning the mechanical ease of casting and retrieving masks a great deal of rather inadequate fishing.

In spinning we try to present a swimming bait, such as a devon, in such a way that a salmon will take it (for reasons not very clear to any of us). Usually, the salmon will take the bait presented to it in its lie. Thus, accurate casting and good fishing presentation are essential. Think of the devon as you would a sunk fly. You must not only be able to reach the area in which the salmon are lying but the devon must have recovered from the cast and be swimming properly, at the right speed and angle, when it comes into the view of the salmon.

The effect of the cast is overcome most quickly by taking up the slack line (if any) and getting in touch with your bait as soon as you can. On windy days a difficult belly upstream may be formed during the cast and it is usually necessary to wind in fairly rapidly until this is taken up. A common fault, even among experienced anglers, is to overdo this part of getting in touch with your bait, and the result is that the devon suddenly speeds up and is drawn off the lie too quickly.

Watch a devon from a bridge, your own if possible, and you will see why wind and good spinning are extremely difficult to reconcile. I was once watching my devon behaving from a bridge when a salmon took it. I know now why the bait suddenly became attractive to the fish. The devon was cast well downstream, as it usually is from a bridge, and began fishing the moment it struck the water. It hovered, swimming at a slow, steady pace for a few seconds without my retrieving it at all and a salmon that I didn't know about materialised from the bottom, took it solidly and was duly landed.

A long rod helps enormously in good spinning. I have moved up in the last ten years or so from a 9ft cane rod to a 9ft 6in one, and finally to a 10ft glass one. I like the extra control this gives me in holding line up over intervening streams and letting the devon explore the apron beyond the fast water. This is a particularly rewarding lie when fish are running and you see salmon showing in the calm water beyond the neck of a stream. It may be a long cast and there may be broken water in between that would pull your bait off course rapidly.

I remember one most successful day on the right bank of Delagyle on the Spey (near Aberlour), where the fish were lying in that lovely holding apron of the stream opposite the hut on the Wester Elchies side. By standing high on the path on the Delagyle side I was able to hold the devon with a high rod point for five or even ten seconds before the stream drew the bait off the lie too quickly. I had four fish in succession, and all took because the longer rod helped me to control the devon at fairly long range.

A spinning reel, whether it be a fixed-spool reel or a multiplier, has always seemed to me to be a device for retrieving line after the interesting part of the fishing is over. I exaggerate, of course, but with point. Grinding in immediately after casting, as if the retrieving action is always necessary for fishing the bait, is the commonest fault in spinning. Of course, there are times when you want to move your bait in a little more quickly than others, and there are certainly cases where you want urgently to move the bait before letting it hover, but in general it is better to let the devon land, right itself and fish round with the current, just as a fly would, than to retrieve line in the early stages of the fishing out of a cast.

This technique of casting and holding the bait to let the current fish it round is more typical of the faster streams of the middle and upper Spey than of the slower pools of the lower Tay. But even there the current is often perfectly adequate for the technique. Those who wade the Tay will agree with me that the glides and pool tails are often far faster than they seem from the bank. The Spey has more boulders and shows streams more clearly—from Grantown down, anyway.

The baits with which this swinging lure is best fished are the wooden devons common on the Tay and on Speyside, and certain of the Toby spoons, chiefly the larger but lighter ones—i.e. the $\frac{5}{8}$oz—suits the technique better than either the $\frac{3}{4}$oz or 1oz baits. The method I use for weighting my devons is also relevant to the swinging-lure type of spinning. I use a spiral above the ball-bearing swivel on the trace, which is 3ft above the devon at a maximum. I screw the spiral into the eye of the swivel and bend the lead to form a safe anti-kink device. This lead will ride on the bottom in deep spring work and allow the lighter devon to follow the current attractively. The trace, weighted thus, can be cast good distances, although I recognise the aerodynamic problems associated with the rig, especially the bolas effect. Heavier devons, however, do not swim with the sensitivity I want. Further, the lead up the trace is a great bottom-finder but not a bad bottom-snagger. A metal devon that bumps the bottom usually also sticks.

I moved off fixed-spool reels for Spey and Tay spinning with 2in to 3in devons—i.e. spring spinning baits—more than a decade ago, and I would find it a rather odd experience to spin for long with the fixed-spool. This is a personal point, of course, and a constant topic of discussion between myself and my 'fixed-spool' friends, many of whom are expert salmon fishers. I have in fact isolated myself by two stages from the fixed-spool reel. I have for six years been fishing a multiplier, which has an optional free spool for long casting or rotating handle arrangement for direct drum contact with the devon as it is spinning or with fish being played. Indeed, when I hook a fish on my 10ft glass rod and have the fish turn the drum and the handles of the reel during the fight, it is an experience not too far away from playing a fish on fly tackle.

One of the things I am not at all sure about in spinning, even after fishing for salmon for some twenty-five years, is whether the fish on a given stream want the bait with its head upstream or presented more or less sideways on. I usually try a first run through the pool assuming the head-upstream presentation, but a second run gives the opportunity to try a more square cast and a shorter hovering period before the stream sweeps the bait round.

The Toby spoon fishes beautifully in a sideways presentation on some broad Tay streams and I have evidence from the hooking positions that salmon seize this long bait across the middle as it crosses their lies. Devons are much more typically seized either in a turning swirl, which hooks the fish inside the mouth at the angle of the jaw, or by that difficult offer, the snatch from behind. Toby baits taken across the middle often result in the fish being hooked in the angle of the jaw from outside. This can lead to an insecure hold when the bait comes out of the fish's mouth during the fight and has strain applied to the hook-hold from the opposite direction to that of original hooking. When people talk of losing fish on the Toby I nearly always point to this problem associated with large baits that can be taken across the middle by salmon in streams.

I have to admit that raw beginners to salmon fishing seldom take fish consistently on fly, but do so in many cases with spinning gear. The ease of casting and the simplicity of certain kinds of spinning make this a possibility for many beginners. But consistent catches on spinning gear from a wide variety of water demand a great deal of good watercraft and careful handling of tackle. I sometimes think that those who look down their noses at fish we catch on devons must assume that there is only one form of spinning, the limited cast—grind—recover form. Years of fishing throughout Scotland have taught me that spinning has its range of skills just as fly fishing has, and that the average angler is misled if he thinks beginner's luck sums up the method.

December 1972   *Bill Currie*

'Hands' and the cast

Captain Tommy Edwards once said to me, 'All good casting is the same action. It's only the plane that varies, and it doesn't matter whether it's fly or bait, single or double-handed.'

It took me some time to absorb and inwardly digest that remark. As always with that great fisherman and caster, it was the distillate of years of experience put into its most simple form. Tommy was perpetually teaching simple truths, which many of us, wrapped up in the techniques of power and distance, were apt to forget. He had an uncanny knack of pinpointing a simple casting fault that was spoiling the whole casting action. He watched your hands.

I have often thought how beautifully simple and true was his method of linking all three types of casting into one basic action. His theory was that the double-handed salmon cast was nothing more than a single-handed trout cast, with the left hand added to the butt

Action of the overhead cast. The right hand is gripping the rod lightly, and the left hand is following and supporting the butt, which pendulums in and out under the heart

of the longer rod to support it, and to follow it passively. The bait or spinning cast also is nothing more than a single-handed fly cast in an inclined plane with a turn of the hips to smooth it out.

Don't believe it? Well try this little experiment. Take the butt section of a rod, or any straight piece of wood 3–4ft long—a broom handle will do. Hold it about halfway along its length and make a simple overhead trout cast with it. The butt part beneath the casting hand will pendulum backwards and forwards beneath the casting forearm.

Now incline the 'rod' slightly to the right (if you are casting with your right hand). The butt will now be penduluming in and out beneath your left breast. Put your left hand on to the bottom of the butt to support it lightly, and follow it, in and out from beneath your left breast, for some six inches or so of forward and backward travel. There you are doing a double-handed salmon fly cast.

Keep this movement going, but incline the 'rod' tip more towards the ground, until it's a little more than 45 degrees from the vertical. Now add a smooth twisting movement with the hips only, turning back as the rod goes back and forwards as the rod goes forward. Now you are doing a double-handed bait cast. Take off the left hand from the butt, and there is the single-handed bait cast. The action is the same throughout. Only the plane of the rod is different.

The truth of these ideas is seen if you watch the hands of a good caster. They follow the same course for all types of cast, but with the right hand changing its plane. The left hand moves out from under the left side of the chest for about 6in, pauses while the line flies over the rod tip and straightens behind, then moves in again under the heart.

The right arm bends at the elbow, then at the wrist on the back cast, then flicks forward or uncocks at the wrist, and partly straightens at the elbow on the forward cast. The elbow should not move forward, but may move up and down. This is all done in or near to the vertical in the fly casts, and on an inclined plane for the bait casts.

If you have used a rod butt to try all this with, then you'll follow it that much more easily. There are minor variations, I agree, but Captain Edwards' message was that the basic action is simple and the same for all.

In their classic book *The Anglers' Cast*, Eric Horsfall Turner and Captain Edwards stressed the importance of 'hands', as well as the inherent simplicity in casting. This method is so easily seen when demonstrated, but so wordy when put to type. I sometimes think that we have lost sight of this simplicity in casting, especially when I see the laboured and exaggerated antics of some of my reservoir friends. They huff and they puff and they haul the line out by ungainly brute force. In contrast, watch Don Neish double-hauling.

It's all so smooth and easy, with a short, sharp power arc; the rest of the rod's travel is drift.

Don is another who, like myself, was lucky enough to count Captain Edwards as a friend and London neighbour. His style reflects it. Tommy could power-cast, drift and double-haul with the best of them—and I mean the world's best—but it never looked strenuous, ugly or laboured. The line flowed easily, smoothly and majestically for him, and went 'miles'! It was all built up on this simple basic action I have just described.

These methods of casting are still being taught on the courses at Grantown-on-Spey. Captain Edwards ran them for nearly twenty years, and was joined by Arthur Ogelsby for the last twelve years. Arthur has now taken over as instructor-in-charge, and is carrying on Captain Edwards' methods of casting. I count myself lucky to have been at Grantown when Tommy was teaching on his courses. I learned more in an hour watching him 'at work', fault-finding and fault-eliminating, than I would have in a year of self-tuition.

So remember his advice the next time you see someone casting. Forget the rod and line, and watch the action of his hands. You'll soon see where his faults lie, and probably some of your own as well.

October 1970   *Alastair Perry*

Piping in the salmon

The small kirk of St Fergus, at Dalarossie in Inverness-shire, stands miles from the main road, on a promontory overlooking the Findhorn. There could hardly be a more beautiful site: it stands in isolation, its granite walls and slated roof flanked on two sides by farmland and on the other two by the river. Its well-kept churchyard is surrounded by a sturdy stone dyke, over which the tall tombstones gaze sternly, like chessmen, into the river 10yd below.

Under their gaze is a salmon pool, named, I need hardly add, Church Pool, in which salmon rest before tackling the tumbling, fast-running water, which turns through a right-angle round the point on which the church stands. The church is little used these days. The ruins of crofts and school bear witness to the size of the former population of the glen, now alas, long gone.

But last September, there was a rare event at the church—a wedding. No ordinary wedding, either, but that of a local laird, which had brought guests from all over the county. The church holds a mere seventy-two people, and there was an overflow of guests waiting outside. My wife and I were fishing the opposite bank of the Findhorn and for once the water was almost perfect after a spate and there was a tremendous run of autumn salmon. During the morning we had had four fish, and just before lunch I had beaten our previous family record with a fish of 17½lb. Considering my advancing years, I was convinced that my fish would retain the record for the remainder of our fishing lives!

We went up to the Church Pool just after two o'clock in the afternoon. I went to the head of the pool and started fishing where the white water broke round the bend and my wife went further down to fish the tail. For a short while we fished, listening to the rush of the water and the dimly-heard murmur of the marriage service only 25yd away on the other bank, when suddenly there was a screech from my wife, which might well have startled the minister, and she was into a big fish that had taken with enthusiasm her size 6 double-hooked Garry Dog.

The screech was loud enough to be heard by the waiting wedding guests on the opposite bank, and in no time at all there was an interested audience, with buttonholes and wedding hats, leaning on the churchyard wall and watching the battle below!

My wife succeeded in stoppping the fish from going out of the tail of the pool, into a rushing torrent full of boulders, where she would surely have lost him and kept him trying to fight his way upstream, against the strong current. Twice, by sheer brute force, he pulled his way to the head of the pool and got his nose into the white water foaming over the rocks, and twice, with her heart in her mouth, she forced him to turn his head and back away before he could cut the cast on a sharp rock face.

The banks of the pool are steep and the water deep, and a fish is difficult to gaff or net unless one can get out to a sandy spit near the tail, to which a tired fish can be led. I just managed to reach this spit without getting wet, when, after twenty minutes of unrelenting struggle, my wife relaxed the pressure and let the tiring fish drop downstream. I was ready with the net in the water, and as he drifted slowly back, I had him in it. The subdued and decorous cheers from the spectators opposite were much appreciated.

I waded gingerly back, carrying in the net what I could feel at once was the heaviest fish either of us had every caught, a great cock fish with a kype like a rhinocerous horn! I staggered up the bank and, having despatched him, hung him on my spring balance. He weighed just 18½lb. My unbeatable family record had lasted just two hours!

'Well done,' said I to my wife, as I held the fish up in the air, 'I wish we had some way to celebrate this.'

As I spoke, as if waiting for the cue, the doors of the church opposite were thrown open, and the bride and bridegroom emerged preceded by a piper, whose joyful music came singing across the water to us. His music was for the happiness of the new husband and wife, but it could not have been more appropriate for us at that moment. It was a wonderful moment, and the nicest wish my wife and I could think to send to the bride and bridegroom was that in their married life they may often experience such moments of happiness, excitement and success, all combined. Certainly, we are grateful to them for, fortuitously, providing the pipe music at exactly the right moment. It crowned the occasion for us, and made it one we shall certainly never forget.

March 1976   *J F Todhunter*

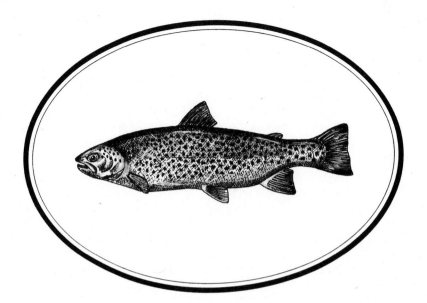

Sea-Trout

The puzzle of the sea-trout's feeding

Results of scientific investigations show conclusively that the adult salmon does not feed on its return to the river. However, whether adult sea-trout similarly restrict their feeding activities while in freshwater has never been satisfactorily determined.

Although several workers have shown that sea-trout are active and varied feeders in coastal and estuarine waters, accounts of their diet while in the river are scarce and generally based upon a small number of observations from restricted localities.

G H Nall, the great authority on sea-trout, examined the stomachs of fish caught above the limits of the tide. He investigated the diet of 150 sea-trout from Loch Maree and recorded the presence of a bumble bee, wasps, water beetles, small land beetles, various insects and small crustaceans, but no fish, in their stomachs. From this and observations in other areas, Nall concluded that sea-trout, both clean and kelts, taken in the sea and in tidal waters, are at times gorged with food, but that in freshwater this is rarely so.

I recently had the opportunity to examine the stomachs of 150 sea-trout from the Afon Dyfi (Dovey) in mid-Wales. Two-thirds of these fish were caught at night by fly fishing and more than half were caught during July and August. The fish ranged in size from 4oz to 9lb; forty-five (39 per cent) were males and seventy-one (61 per cent) were females. All were caught at least two-and-a-half miles above the tidal limits. None bore sea-lice and their general condition indicated that they had all been in the river for several weeks.

Food occurred in only thirty-eight (25 per cent) and was absent in 112 (75 per cent) of the stomachs.

Among the animals occurring in the diet of Dyfi sea-trout were worms, shrimps, stonefly larvae, caddis larvae, midge larvae and adults, beetles, earwigs, wood ants, millipedes, spiders, moths and fish.

The results obtained from the Dyfi differed in certain respects from those obtained from Loch Maree. Whereas fish were absent from the diet of Loch Maree sea-trout, two Dyfi fish had eaten salmon and trout parr. Nall grouped his Loch Maree sea-trout into four categories based upon the various amounts of food found in their stomachs—'much', 'moderate', 'little' and 'no' food.

Comparison shows that the Dyfi sea-trout had fed far less extensively than those from Loch Maree. While 38 per cent of the Loch Maree fish contained 'much' or 'moderate' amounts of food, only 2 per cent of the Dyfi fish were in these two categories: 98 per cent of the Dyfi sea-trout contained 'little' or 'no' food in their stomachs.

It was interesting that food occurred in only five of the 101 stomachs of rod-caught fish. In this respect it seems that the sea-trout, like salmon, is not necessarily feeding when it takes a fly or lure.

The Dyfi is not a good brown trout river, but it was possible to examine the diet of eighteen fish caught over the same period as the sea-trout. All the brown trout stomachs were more than half full with a variety of terrestrial and aquatic insects, showing that, unlike the sea-trout, they had been extensively feeding.

All Nall's material came from within Loch Maree. No fish were obtained from the River Ewe. Therefore, his results may not be typical of sea-trout feeding under normal river conditions. The freshwater diet of Dyfi sea-trout was less extensive than that recorded from Loch Maree, but generally supported the view expressed by Nall that: 'There is little doubt that after leaving saltwater, sea-trout feed more intermittently and with a less robust appetite than brown trout.'

If we accept that sea-trout do feed in freshwater, then it would be interesting to discover the extent to which they are dependent upon obtaining a source of nourishment while in the river for their eventual survival. Survival among sea-trout kelts is far greater than among salmon kelts. I have read scales from Dyfi sea-trout that have indicated that as many as eight spawnings have been survived, and more than 40 per cent of the stocks of Dyfi sea-trout consists of fish that have spawned at least once.

Rarely does the salmon survive to spawn twice, the majority of salmon and grilse dying after they have spawned for the first time. Does this better survival among sea-trout after spawning result from their feeding and taking in nourishment while in the river, thereby limiting the demands made upon their body reserves, so that they are

better able to survive the journey back to a rich and plentiful supply of food in the sea? Or is it that sea-trout kelts, unlike salmon kelts, do not linger in the river after spawning?

Another interesting question is, if sea-trout do feed in freshwater and if this is necessary for their survival, why are not more sea-trout caught during the day? Do they feed actively only between the hours of dusk and dawn? Surely, in the river, where the food supply is severely limited compared with the sea, they would be expected to feed whenever food was available, regardless of the time of day. Consequently, their capture in daylight should be a more common occurrence. Why is it that sea-trout are more vulnerable to night fishing? Why aren't more salmon caught at night?

Although the scientific evidence is limited, it seems that the sea-trout, unlike the salmon, may feed while in freshwater, but to a much lesser extent than the brown trout. However, more extensive scientific investigation into the diet of adult sea-trout from other waters in the British Isles is required before generalisations about the nature and extent of their feeding can be made. Information supplied by a number of anglers in the West Country has suggested that, in that area, the freshwater feeding of adult sea-trout may be more extensive than in either the Dyfi or Loch Maree. Certainly, a greater proportion of the fish appear to have food in their stomachs.

April 1972   *Graeme Harris*

The unpredictable fish

In salmon fishing there can be found a pattern of behaviour that, variable as it may be, makes it possible to fish in a particular way at particular times with at least average possibilities of success. The sea-trout, however, is so unpredictable that chances and methods of catching it vary from day to day and, most particularly, from river to river.

I have fished in coloured water seething with sea-trout in conditions that should have been ideal, and caught none. I have hooked fish in bright sunshine in gin-clear water that I have assumed to be salmon but that, when landed, have turned out to be sea-trout. I have caught them when fishing upstream in low water for brown trout—yet have frequently failed to make any contact while night fishing in perfect circumstances.

Real implacable local experts have urged me to use small flies, while, on the same river, men equally expert have derided such a theory and declared one's chances hopeless without flies nearly large enough for February on the Tweed. On one occasion while fishing for salmon in the Deveron, in conditions perfect for salmon and fishing only in their taking places, I ended the day with eight sea-trout weighing 24lb—and no salmon. I did not complain at such sport, but felt somehow that it was undeserved.

Only twice, as far as I can remember, have I been broken by salmon when fly fishing for them, though good fortune may have a heavy bearing on this. I can think of half a dozen occasions when strong nylon has parted like cotton when I have been sea-trout fishing. There are, of course, sea-trout in such rivers as the Conway and the Dovey that make many salmon look, in comparison, like babies. But this is not the whole story. The truth is that a big sea-trout is, in the ordinary way, harder to catch than a salmon.

In most rivers one's best chance of the big sea-trout lies in night fishing—one of the most stimulating and exhausting forms of torture that any fisherman can inflict on himself! To achieve perfect conditions the temperature should be high and the water low. This means one thing. It means summer and long, light evenings.

Continuous casting at an invisible target at the other side of the black river is a test for anyone's skill and nerves, especially with two flies on the cast and a line that tends eventually to become waterlogged. When an invisible hand seems suddenly to emerge from the water and pull at the flies, anything can happen—particularly when the night sounds have been accompanied by crashes and splashes in the target area that put one in mind of a school of dolphins at play. The strike may have been ill-timed or there may have been countless wind knots in the nylon, but the ease with which the submarine to which one appears to have become briefly attached throws off its shackles is frequently depressing and always impressive.

Though the built-in perils of night fishing can account for some of the disasters, there can be no argument that a fresh-run sea-trout gives, pound for pound, a more ferocious struggle than any of the salmon and brown-trout family (except perhaps an equally fresh-run grilse). The hazards are increased by the softness of a sea-trout's mouth, which seems to me to be built specially to discourage a firm-hold.

I never cease to be astonished at the power of even quite small fish. Last summer in low water but at the head of a fast pool, I hooked a fish that I took immediately to be a salmon. Keeping a firm hold on it but hardly shifting it from the place where it took, I backed carefully to dry land. At that stage the fish decided to run, tore downstream and jumped. It turned out to be a sea-trout that weighed 2½lb. No other fish of that size could have held its own against the pull of a 12ft salmon rod for so long.

On some salmon rivers, of course, sea-trout are regarded as being close to vermin. There is a justified feeling that catching one is apt to disturb a pool and reduce the chances of a salmon. And I have dispatched sea-trout and salmon to friends simultaneously. The salmon have arrived in good condition and the sea-trout have arrived spoiled.

But perhaps the greatest drawback of all is the hammering a fisherman takes when he is fishing on a river with good stocks of both salmon and sea-trout. If he is on holiday, full of the energy of the man who does not get enough fishing in the other fifty weeks of the year, he will find himself slogging for the salmon by day and beating himself hard after the sea-trout by night.

He is liable in such circumstances to return to work badly in need of a soothing rest cure at some quiet, peaceful and riverless resort—and possibly, too, of legal advice to cope with the cries of a wife who has seen him only at breakfast time.

May 1969   *David Barr*

Fishing by night . . .

There is a charm about night fishing for sea-trout that few other sports can give. But the conditions must be right. First it must not be too dark. I have heard men say 'the darker the better'. I am sure this is wrong. If one of these 'darker-the-better' men were taken out on a really dark January night and told to fish, he would agree. Fortunately at the season when night fishing is most successful—15 June to 31 July—it is seldom very dark in Scotland. Then the night should be still; perhaps a light breeze does no harm and may disperse some of the midge hoards, but a strong or fresh wind destroys the fishing.

The night angler should if possible select his water where he knows there are fish and confine himself to that place. It is a mistake to wander up and down a river bank or to go plunging about in the river when its bed is hidden. Such action only scares the fish or leads the angler to a ducking.

It is as well to make up two or three casts with the fly attached in the comfort of the home. It is easier to tie on a fresh cast than a new fly in the dark, even with the aid of a torch.

At night flies can, with advantage, be one or two sizes bigger and casts heavier. One fly to a cast is ample and reduces the chance of entanglement.

If it is available, sea-trout will drop back into shallower water at night and good fish can be caught in water only a few inches deep.

I think it is a mistake to begin fishing too early, indeed the light should have dwindled beyond the point where you can see the fly land upon the water. Some anglers tell me that they find difficulty in casting smoothly and accurately at night. I think this is partly due to unfamiliarity with the conditions, but one tip is worth following for those that are beset with doubts about their casting. Imagine that the water surface is 2ft higher than it is in reality and cast as if this were so. This saves the splashy entry and even if it shortens the cast by a yard or so, it is better to lose this distance rather than to scare fish.

Move slowly when wading at night. Apart from the risk of a tumble or the sounds of hobnail boots on stones, waves caused by staggered paces are disturbing, and you are more likely to stagger in shallow water than you are in deep water.

On hooking a fish do not be in too great a hurry to come ashore, wait till the first violence of the contest is over if the conditions allow this to be done. Of course there are times when you have to come out quickly in order to follow a wild fish that has taken you up or down. After a successful contest do not think that because the water has been lashed by the struggles of the fish the remaining fish will not take. They soon recover and more fish can be taken within a short time from the same spot.

At night the angler has to depend more upon feel than upon sight. The rise is seldom seen, but at times it can be heard and always felt. The necessity of having to depend on two senses, instead of three, is apt to make the excitable angler too hasty or violent in tightening on a fish. The sea-trout that takes at night is much more bent on seizing the fly than he is by day; perhaps the fleeting moment accounts for this phenomenon, so that as a rule he hooks himself. After the hooking you can be as hard as your tackle will stand and no harm should come of it. The danger lies in the initial hooking.

I am not sure that night fishing is such a fine art as fishing by day, but it is the greatest fun and full of exciting and mysterious moments—the tug of an unseen and unknown fish is a peculiarly emotional sensation. The expression 'chuck and chance it' is perhaps more applicable to the night angler than to the daylight wet-fly angler for whom the phrase was first coined.

Many men will spend the whole night fishing. If you like doing this there is no objection, but in my experience fish are responsive for about an hour in the first part of the night and perhaps for about twenty minutes before dawn. The rest of the time is useless. I cannot say just when the optimum moment arrives when the sea-trout take, and I am sure the moment varies; but what makes for this variation escapes me.

If after a warm wet day a white mist can be seen arising from the water, it is useless to continue fishing. Mist puts the fish down more surely than any other condition, apart from a blizzard. This mist has a peculiar miasmic effect rather like floating in a nightmare of cotton wool. The moment I see it I pack up and go home.

If it is a loch that is to be fished at night, even greater care in navigation is called for than by day, with no splashing and the slowest of gentle oarsmanship. As the night will probably be still, the boat will not drift, so some propulsion is required to enable the angler to cover fresh water. It is this gentle movement of the boat that requires the boatman's constant care.

Sea-trout in a loch behave differently from the same fish in a river. They do not take up one stance and stay there. In a loch they cruise and it is the cruising fish you wish to see your fly. In their cruising they will travel to shallower parts of the loch, maybe to the shore or the edges of weed beds, and these places are always worth trying. A sea-trout may like the edge of the weed, but at night I do not think that when hooked he will run in to them—as he may do by day. At night he prefers open water.

At night on a loch there is no need for long casting. If the boat is well handled sea-trout will take your fly quite close to it. But remember, with a short line much of the elasticity is gone and the action of the rod is communicated to the fly more quickly so that a sharp strike becomes almost a blow.

As the season advances night fishing becomes less productive and by the second half of August true night fishing is over, but evening or dusk fishing can replace it.

I would not wish to have all my fishing confined to the darker hours, but even if it requires less skill and more physical dexterity most of us can look back upon many happy hours thus employed.

December 1957   *R N Stewart*

. . . And by day

Fly fishing for sea-trout is a generally accepted nocturnal pastime. This fact is apt to upset non-fishing hotel proprietors, ever-loving wives, fellow guests and others who like an uninterrupted night's sleep. It reduces the hotel's bar takings and limits opportunities to air past triumphs. In short, the nocturnal angler is looked upon as a sort of anti-social nut.

It may be heresy to say that sea-trout can be caught freely during daytime in low water at average summer levels, and, what is more, can be taken in hot weather under a blazing sun.

But let us first consider our adversary. It tends to shoal, has truly exceptional eyesight and lies often in fast streamy water. Many sea-trout are hooked and lost by fishers using small flies, such losses being put down to large trout, as they usually occur in the initial run.

The method and tackle I have found to be effective can be summed up as follows: a 10ft rod, floating line, plenty of backing, and long casting. Casts should be not less than 4yd long, tapered 9lb to 7lb to 5lb.

The most important factor to success, however, is the end product—the fly. Whether you use double or treble hooks is immaterial, but the treble is preferred. Use size 14 or 16 hooks and go as far as 12 only if the water is high. You will be surprised how small a fly a sea-trout can see. The treble hook should be dressed lightly with a darkish hair hackle, a few golden pheasant fibres or jungle cock, and gold and silver wire round the shank.

Exact details of the fly are not critical as long as it is lightly dressed, small and dark in general appearance. The effect to be aimed at should be a rather tattered blob of black hair, relieved with the gold or silver wire on the shank peeping through. This will give amateur fly tyers plenty of room to experiment. Size is vital.

Sea-trout can see these tiny morsels in rough, boulder-strewn streams. They take with a bang and a run that usually brings up the backing to view. Hold the rod well up and let the fish have its head; when it slows down of its own accord and only then, get into a position to manoeuvre it into shallow water.

Be assured that this method will catch sea-trout on a hot July or August day and do not be stampeded into using the more often advised size 8. Even in big water size 12 works well.

In view of the fish's exceptional eyesight, long casting is a must. Fish as you would the greased-line for salmon; let the fly come right round, mend where necessary and, whatever you do, keep the rod up at an angle of 45 degrees while the fly is coming round.

This method has served me well for at least ten seasons on Scottish rivers, and, in spite of the main quarry being sea-trout, has accounted for a number of salmon. Hooking them is one thing, landing them is another. Nevertheless, you can always land them again in the bar instead of crawling around in the dark retrieving a fly from a bush that was certainly not there in the afternoon!

April 1970 *K J W Hall*

Their various moods

Hamish Stuart wrote: 'The only way to conquer the moods of sea-trout is to ignore them.' However, this is the advice of perfection. It argues that the angler has not only a superlative fishing technique but also the supreme confidence that will win him fish when they are not in taking mood.

Given these two great assets it is true that we can catch sea-trout no matter what mood they are in. Most of us would have to admit, however, that the moods of sea-trout sometimes beat us. When fish refuse to take—even when we spare no effort—many anglers feel disappointment and then experience a lack of confidence in themselves. Some fish defiantly, even carelessly. This only makes the situation worse.

In general terms the moods of sea-trout are governed partly by the relative freshness or staleness of the fish and partly by the condition of the water—whether it is low or medium or spate. The weather—particularly the temperature—must be taken into account too.

When a fresh sea-trout enters a river from the sea its moods pass through two distinct phases. For a short time—varying from a few hours up to a day or so—it reacts like a sea fish. It lies in open water, one of a shoal, and feeds greedily. The chemical change of osmosis appears to sharpen the appetite of fish. Fresh-run sea-trout are almost invariably in a taking mood. In September I found myself casting over a shoal of fresh fish on the lower Towy. The fish took steadily and were still taking when I left for home four hours later. The experience is not uncommon.

The second phase—what may be called the 'growing stale' phase—is the one that presents most of the problems. After a few days in fresh water a sea-trout loses much of its initial sparkle. It begins to feed sporadically—usually at dusk or in the dark. It exhibits an interest in surface and sub-surface insects. Moreover it finds itself a lie or hover to which it can retreat when it is not active. These are the fish that exhibit those negative moods of extreme dourness that tax our skill and patience to its limits. Sometimes, alas, in vain.

It is my personal belief that a healthy sea-trout can nearly always be risen to a fly provided the fly is fished properly. Sea-trout are inordinately fascinated by flies. They will turn at a fly in the most unpromising conditions of light and water. Many such fish have no intention of taking the fly into their mouths. Yet the fact that they have been risen gives the angler a chance to coax or lure them into taking.

Take the case of a shoal of fish lying in a rock gully against a steep bank. Lowish water and the fact that the fish have been upriver for a week weighs against the angler. A standard size fly No.4 (new numbers) will shift a few fish but none is hooked. The fish stir lazily and follow the fly out of curiosity. One or two may rise and actually nibble at the dressing of the fly. Having moved the fish and stirred their interest it may be possible to catch a few by varying the tactics. A small (No.2) Brown Nymph or Black Spider fished slowly, without handlining, is worth a prolonged trial. If this fails, the shoal should be rested and a standard size fly tried once more but from a different angle. Working the two combinations—with rests in between—a capture, sooner or later, is a near certainty.

A feature of game fishing is the way fish seem to sense a coming weather change. Coombe Richards once told me that he believes salmon can detect weather changes some weeks in advance of the event. Sea-trout certainly appear to sense weather changes several days in advance. Fish in low water, for example, often become restive for no observable reason. They exhibit a desire to run and this often takes the form of leaping, usually at the neck of the pool. A slight change, perhaps in the barometic pressure has put them in a travelling mood and food becomes of small account. After an hour or two, this mood often exhausts itself. Wisely, the angler has rested himself and he then finds that fish have fallen back along the pool margins where they are once again interested in fly. In this case the mood of the fish is overridden by patience.

Some anglers fail to exploit the wet fly to its full advantage when after sea-trout. To cast and recover a fly at the same angle and in the same manner at every throw is not the best way of catching a suspicious fish that has lost its saltwater keenness. The angler must try to visualise the fly at the end of his cast and put every effort into making it swim at a pace and in the manner of a creature of relative size.

Handlining is a little understood art at which not everyone is a master. I have proved to my own satisfaction numerous times on the

Towy, Teifi and Cleddau that a fly allowed to drift passively across a pool is not always successful. Nor is a fly that is worked vigorously and regularly. If, however, the angler gives the fly a tiny tug at certain intervals in the drift—the precise moment found by careful trial and error—he will find his basket improved out of all proportion.

Fish are rather like theatre-goers. Put a lamp-post and a few windows on the stage and people will readily imagine they are looking at a city. The angler need only hint that his fly is alive and sea-trout will be eager to deceive themselves.

These and similar tricks make Stuart's dictum substantially true. It might also be true to say, perhaps, that there is no such thing as a non-taking sea-trout—if you know enough about fishing.

January 1960   *F W Holiday*

Types of takes

Most anglers seem to accept the unpredictable and whimsical taking moods of sea-trout as one of nature's insoluble mysteries and as an inevitable facet of this type of fishing. No doubt this adds to its fascination, but I have always felt there must be at least a partial answer to the different ways in which sea-trout, depending on their degree of 'freshness' in the river, on water and air temperature, and perhaps on a host of other factors, attack a fly differently. Over the years I have been intensely interested in sea-trout and their various habits, and I feel that, to a certain extent at any rate, I have evolved methods of reacting to the various types of takes, and now enjoy a greater measure of success than was my lot before I adopted them.

For this purpose I divide sea-trout into three distinct categories, although only the first two are of any consequence. Obviously, it is the type of take to which one must react, not whether it might be a fresh or not-so-fresh fish, but I find this method of classification convenient for stating the case in question.

First, let us consider fresh-run fish that have been in the water for up to about three weeks. Generally speaking, they seize the fly avidly and violently, and there is little one can do about hooking. To retain the hold, however, the rod must be held high, the line kept taut at all times and a fair pressure maintained on the fish. If you do not maintain this pressure, your fly may become unstuck because of the softness of mouth in a fresh-run fish. But if you are too rough on him, you may tear the fly out for the very same reason. My advice is to keep him moving and bring him to the net as soon as possible. But hasten slowly!

Sea-trout that have been in river or loch for more than three weeks and have lost their initial 'bloom' but still provide desirable sport—the second category for our present purpose—are probably the most enigmatic takers of all and present the greatest problem. They seem to be affected by external conditions more than new arrivals and can vary their take from night to night and even from dusk to darkness and again at dawn.

They often accept the fly in quite a positive manner, but immediately come to the surface and thrash wildly until the hook invariably becomes unstuck. I used to lose sea-trout after sea-trout in this manner, and tried every conceivable dodge before finding that the most successful answer to the problem was a fairly simple one: as soon as I feel the pull, I give the fish a couple of feet of line I have left hanging slack, then I quickly bring my rod right up to the vertical, simultaneously winding in as fast as I can. This method doesn't ensure success every time, but I have found it more profitable than any other, and whereas I used to grass perhaps one fish in six that took in this manner, I now manage three or even four of them.

'Plucking' is another common and perplexing taking habit with this type of sea-trout. I have vivid recollections of one summer's night on the Aberdeenshire Dee, near Aboyne, when for an hour, three of us hooked a trout with almost every cast, but the total catch was a single fish. It was the best example of 'plucking' I have known, and it was followed each time by a run in towards the rod. You could hardly wind in fast enough to get all the slack back on to your reel and, when you did, the fish was gone on contact and the fly propelled at lightning speed past your ear or impaled in your jacket or round your legs. That is not exactly a comforting situation when you are out in the water on a dark night!

My answer to 'plucking' is also a simple one, and I have found it on the whole extremely effective. I drop the rod tip almost to water-level, which is the same thing as giving slack line, and strike with a long sideways swing to the left if I am fishing from the left bank and to the right if I am on the right bank. I have yet to find a more telling way of dealing with this peculiar but common type of take.

Sea-trout moving from the second category to the 'stale-fish' group often seem just to stop the fly and hold it, little movement being transmitted along the line to the rod. In such cases I strike firmly as soon as I am aware of the resistance and waste no time in bringing the fish to the net.

Really stale fish—those that have been in fresh water for weeks on end—usually take in the manner just described or, more often, do not take at all. These black fish are not really worth having in any case and are rarely fished for seriously, so that their loss is much less galling to the angler. For the purposes of this article, they are more or less irrelevant.

As for hooks, I am now convinced that size 12 or 14 doubles are, over the season, the most satisfactory. If the fish really opens his mouth, you have a far better chance of gripping him. On the other hand, if he sucks it in without parting his lips much, a single hook is no doubt preferable. To deal with this situation I normally start off with a cast of two doubles and a single, or two singles and a double. If I am catching fish on the single then I change to a complete cast of singles and vice-versa.

To be more successful with the enigmatic sea-trout than the next man, you have to be prepared to adapt your tactics to suit the manner in which the fish are taking on the night in question. These conclusions have been reached by trial and error after many years of fishing and hundreds of nights that all too often produced only an empty or near-empty creel in the morning, and working from the premise that a problem half-solved is better than no solution at all, I shall continue to employ the tactics described here until someone improves upon them. That would indeed be a welcome addition to angling knowhow, since the whimsical sea-trout must also be the most puzzling taker of a fly we can find anywhere.

June 1973 *James Fyfe*

Large flies or small?

Styles in fishing are as susceptible as anything else to the whims of change in fashion that exist in the everyday world, and we often find that one particular method becomes popular for a while, only to wane whenever an alternative temporarily achieves more publicity. The confusion this may cause to the inexperienced angler has never been more evident than in the confusion surrounding the use of a large or small fly when fishing for the first hour or so after dark.

The see-saw argument between the two styles had gone on for years, and the fisherman eager to learn and improve his technique can be thoroughly puzzled when he hears two successful experts fiercely propounding contrasting theories. The situation seems illogical until you start to think for yourself and delve deeper into the problem by examining the whole circumstances. Then one often finds that the two experts fish on rivers of a different type, or one may fish nearer the estuary of the same river than the other, but seldom do they fish the same section.

I would suggest that herein lies the answer to the riddle, as the two methods are not antagonistic as one might have thought. The experienced sea-trout fisher regards them as complementary and will pick the method that, on his assessment of the particular circumstances, is the most likely to be successful.

Let us first consider the large fly or lure school of thought, by which I mean those who use flies or lures of between 1in and 3in. The principles upon which this theory are based must be well-known to most fishermen, but for the sake of this discussion, they well stand a brief reiteration.

In the sea, sea-trout have a variety of food such as shrimps and eels, but the bulk of the diet is probably taken from the shoals of small fish near the surface as the daylight begins to fade. However, feeding as such stops once freshwater is encountered, and most people have by now accepted the fact that food is no longer necessary to the fish from then on. But the pattern of activity when the light begins to fail becomes second nature and will persist for a varying length of time after the fish has entered the river. Consequently a lure of a fish-like shape and size is often readily taken by instinct if presented near the surface when the time of restlessness is upon the sea-trout after dusk.

This is not an active seeking of food, but more of a habit that becomes less pronounced the longer the fish has been in the river and probably disappears within two weeks. Hence, a large lure will be successful in the lower reaches, and well up river, too, if extra water has enabled fresh fish to travel a reasonable distance within a short time. This technique is well understood and so needs no further elaboration here. In low water the progress may have been too slow, the instinct has faded, a large lure is often ignored and so different tactics become necessary.

The use of a small fly—sizes 6 to 12—is based on the theory that the sea-trout loses its saltwater memories and, becoming immersed in its river surroundings, recollects more and more the activity pattern of feeding by the immature fish developing in the river—the parr. Just how strong this motivation becomes is variable, but undoubtedly it is seldom as powerful as that which caused the sea-trout to take a lure when newly arrived from the sea.

As one might expect with such a less well-developed instinct, it is more vulnerable to the inhibiting effects of unsuitable external influences, such as the temperature of the air and water, atmospheric pressure and humidity. This has given rise to a variety of flies and methods, borne of desperation, to overcome the problem, but essentially one is endeavouring to tempt fish by using a compromise 'fly' midway in size between the lure and the natural fly, so utilising what remains of the small fish-taking instinct and the developing memory for natural flies. This is a rather vague premise upon which to base a style of fishing, but it is all one has on the middle reaches of our sea-trout rivers, which are often rather acid in character, with a subsequent dearth of fly-life.

The small-fly technique becomes more successful if the fly-taking memory is stimulated more than usual, and such conditions may arise in those rivers that have an adequate fly-life. The greater the volume of fly activity, the more effective does the method become. Once again, the period after dusk is most productive, but this has no relation to that of the previous style based on saltwater habits. The governing factor is the increase in food supply at that time, either due to flies on the surface or a build-up in the inverterbrate drift.

Research has shown that nymphal activity greatly increases with the change of light, so that more are exposed to the influence of the current and are swept away to the awaiting fish. Indeed, it has been suggested that brown-trout may obtain up to 50 per cent of their daily food at this time, and there is no reason to believe that sea-trout parr are any different. Such quantities of food may be sufficient to stimulate the memories of feeding. This may indeed take place in a desultory fashion, but although active feeding is not essential to the well-being, an artificial fly presented in a suitable size and manner may well provoke a response.

As one might expect, the memory is more easily stimulated in the younger sea-trout that returns from the sea after an absence of about three to four months, unlike the bigger fish that may have been away for a year or more. This adds weight to the adage 'small flies . . . small fish', but a fish of 1½lb can provide excellent sport on suitable tackle and tastes delicious after a brief sojourn in the frying pan. Indeed, the fight from these smaller fish is more reliable, and I suppose we have all been disappointed at times by the occasional dour performance put up by a fish of more than, say, 5lb.

So if one is to fish an unfamiliar river, it is well worth while trying to ascertain the type if we are to make the most of its potential, for rivers vary considerably in character. The famous Dovey in Wales, is an example of an acid river with little fly-life except in the upper reaches, and this, combined with no obstruction to the upward progress of the fish, makes a large lure highly successful over much of the length of the river. A few miles to the south, the Teifi has a good fly population extending to the tidal waters, and so a small fly can be effective just above the estuary if no fresh fish have recently come in and so made the use of a large lure almost obligatory. The Lune, in Lancashire, is a mixture of the two types. In the lower portion a large lure is preferable, but in the middle and upper reaches, where a good fly population exists, the small lure is generally more appropriate.

All this rationale for the size of fly is pertinent only for the first hour or so after dusk. Once the sea-trout have 'gone down' most people would agree that a large lure on a sunk line is the method of choice. But that's another story.

July 1976   *Barry Lloyd*

Flies

Some thoughts on the mayfly

Being the largest of our Ephemeroptera and coming as they do when the whole of the fly fishing world is mad with the excitement of early season, mayflies, and the pursuit of trout with artificials to represent them, provide an annual and fascinating topic.

For my own part I view the mayfly season from several different angles. As a river keeper my first thoughts are for the well-being of the trout. In rivers where mayflies are abundant there is no doubt, providing indeed they are acceptable to trout, that these big insects are a considerable help in putting fish in first-class condition for the rest of the season. They are body builders. One mayfly has more nutrient value than a dozen olives and what is more, when there are big hatches of them a trout expends little of its energy to get a good meal.

The emphasis, however, is on acceptable. Just because a water produces an abundance of mayflies is no reason to assume that trout will eat them. Excepting for the few days when these flies have their

aerial existence, the two years of their lives are spent in the river bed. The value of the insect as a food for trout depends largely on the wholesomeness of its own food supply.

Good mayfly seasons always follow a winter and spring when the river has been subjected to a thorough scouring with flood water. By a good season I mean from the fishing point of view, a season when trout are eager to take the hatching flies and not too choosy about taking artificials. The hatches may not be as abundant as in seasons following a dry winter, but, as a food and attraction, the value is ten times greater. A river bed scoured is a river bed purified. Spates carry away all foul matter that has accumulated in previous years and so for a while before hatching, the mayfly nymphs can feed in first-class environment.

Mayflies can, and do, live where the bottom of a water is exceedingly foul. Doubtless places come to your mind where hatches of flies have been abundant, where in fact hundreds of the insects have appeared on the water yet with scarcely a trout rising. In such places a fish may rise and take two or three flies and then down he goes for the rest of the day. You know a fair stock of trout are in the reach and possibly try to console yourself by assuming these fish are taking nymphs before they reach the surface.

Sometimes indeed this is true, but no nymphing fish will continue to take sub-aqueous mayfly nymphs without occasionally taking one as it is hatching, or a floating fly. Most certainly there will be some indication to show a fish is feeding. No, it is not that the fish are feeding underwater, but the simple fact that neither nymph nor fly is good to eat.

I well remember fishing part of the Hungerford Town water two years ago. It is a wide flat, upstream of a mill. Indeed it is an artificial leat, and as such has been a trap for spoil through generations. The current is sluggish and the bed muddy almost from bank to bank. Here thousands of mayflies hatched in a couple of hours yet, except for one small grayling, not a fish moved. There were plenty of trout, and big trout, in the reach. This was proved shortly afterwards when they rose very well to spinners in the evening.

To be quite honest I think it is just nonsense when fishermen say trout become surfeited with mayflies. If this is so, how can one account for the fact that in a certain reach, trout will disregard the nymphs and the hatching flies yet may feed eagerly on a fall of spent which comes very soon after. It cannot be that they get hungry in so short a time. My personal view is that trout will continue to take these insects day after day if they are hatching from a clean river, but in instances such as the one I have described, the flies are acceptable only after they have changed to the perfect creature. Perhaps in sloughing their nymphal and sub-imago skins and in starving a day or two while in aerial form, the creatures lose their unwholesome taste.

The excitement of mayfly time grips me as it does most of us. When occasional fishermen tell me they hate the mayfly, I find it hard to believe. Nature sends us these big and beautiful insects at a time when a river valley is at its best. There is a joy in all surroundings and a thousand things of interest. What more can one wish for than a rise of trout that only the mayfly can bring, the sight of big heads poking through the surface and the thought that each pool, run or eddy, may hold the fish of a lifetime.

To me it is the season for the beginner, it is a time when the aged have a fair chance of competing with the young and more agile, a time in fact when all can enjoy being at the riverside. For me the fascination can never fade and as each season passes I am left with plenty to ponder over.

May 1956   *Frank Sawyer*

The black gnat

In an earlier article I mentioned the belief held by some anglers that trout prefer dark flies to pale ones, citing the iron blue as an example. The black gnat lends further support to this theory, for despite its small size the fish usually welcome its appearance with great enthusiasm.

Moreover, when, as often happens, it appears in large numbers, even those large trout that are seldom seen except in mayfly times are liable to be tempted by its attractions. And because, when they have settled down to a feast of black gnats, the trout frequently ignore everything else, the fly fisherman should never be without a suitable artificial or he may miss a Heaven-sent opportunity.

Fly fishing during a heavy fall of black gnats calls for considerable patience, coupled with precision of casting. The trout station themselves in places where the current brings a steady supply of the insects over their heads and seldom deviate from their chosen positions, since this would be an unnecessary waste of energy.

They do not by any means take every specimen which comes over them, but pick out one every so often with a deliberate and purposeful rise, and if you watch a feeding fish for a few minutes you will probably notice that it rises at regularly spaced intervals.

Instead of casting at random, therefore, it pays to note these intervals and then to endeavour to place your fly immediately in front of your quarry at the moment you judge that it is due to take the next natural. Even so, you may well have to spend some considerable time over each individual fish.

When they are feeding steadily on black gnats, trout do not seem to be easily scared, so unless you perpetrate one of the grosser errors, perseverance usually meets with its reward sooner or later.

Black gnats, being land-bred insects, may be found on any type of water, both running and static. Their season extends from April to September, but I have encountered them most frequently in May and August, and have occasionally seen trout taking them during a hatch of mayflies. They are said to prefer warm, muggy days but I have not noticed this preference myself and the angler should be prepared for them in any kind of weather throughout the fishing season.

Being small and lying flat on the surface, they are easily overlooked, but the sight of a cloud of small dark insects gyrating above the stream or lake will serve as a useful pointer. These must not, however, be confused with silverhorns, small dark sedge-flies that behave in a somewhat similar manner but that are seldom eaten by trout.

For many years the black gnat was identified as *Bibio johannis*, a land-bred dipteran whose name derives from the belief (in my experience an erroneous one) that it appears most frequently around St John the Baptist's day, 24 June. Nowadays, however, it is recognised that the name black gnat covers several species of the order Diptera (two-winged flies) of similar habits and appearance, but for practical purposes it will be sufficient to consider *B. johannis* as the type.

It is an old quip that the black gnat is neither black nor a gnat, but the male, at all events, is dark enough to give the impression of being black, while I do not think we need quibble unduly over the precise definition of a gnat.

The life cycle consists of four stages—egg, larva, pupa and adult—of which the first three are spent entirely on land, though generally in the vicinity of water.

The larvae, which resemble small maggots, live at the roots of various plants, where they subsequently pupate, and on emergence the adults congregate in swarms above the banks or surface of the adjacent lake or river.

Mating takes place in the air. After this some of the females return to the shore to lay their eggs, while others, together with their mates, fall into the water, sometimes while they are still paired. These unfortunate ones then float helpless on the surface, unable to escape from the attention of the waiting fish.

Both sexes have pale iridescent wings, which are carried flat over the back and diverging towards their tips when at rest, like those of the common house fly. The male has a slender cylindrical body, while that of the female is much stouter and more or less egg-shaped, so that there is no difficulty in distinguishing between them.

As they lie on the water their wings are sometimes outstretched on either side like those of a spent spinner, while in other specimens they remain folded over the back.

During a big fall of black gnats the trout have so many opportunities of inspecting the natural insects at close range that a really good imitation is necessary in order to achieve success. Unfortunately, the average commercial pattern falls lamentably short of the required standard, being dressed with upright wings like a dun, and in some cases even possessing long tails!

Halford, who dressed two patterns representing the male and female, went so far as to tie his wings on the slant, but even so the feathers lay in the vertical plane, instead of flat along the body.

A number of amateur fly dressers have since tried their hands at imitating the black gnat, one of the most successful being J W Dunne, the author of *Sunshine and the Dry Fly*, whose pattern represents the female of the species. But as this necessitates the use of a special kind of silk, and in any case I dislike silk for the bodies of dry flies, I have evolved a modified version of his dressing, using the same wings but with a different body and darker hackle.

My pattern, suggesting the male, has proved extremely successful in practice, and a friend of mine, for whom I once tied a few specimens, is so well pleased with it that he has frequently called for fresh supplies to replace losses. I give the full dressing below.

Body A strand from the bronze-black part of a turkey's tail feather

Wings A mixed bunch of green and magenta hackle fibres, in the proportion of about twenty of the former to ten of the latter. These are tied in so as to lie flat along the body, their tips being cut into the shape of a V above the bend of the hook

Hackle Black cock, wound over the roots of the wings

Hook 000.

As I have found it difficult to procure black hackles with long stems and short fibres, I use a hackle that is rather too large for the fly and clip the points short after winding. This procedure, I know, was considered an act of vandalism by the older school of fly dressers, but it makes an uncommonly good floater.

By way of variation this pattern might be dressed with wings in the spent position, but as the trout seem perfectly satisfied with my original version I have not found it necessary to make further experiments.

Some anglers use a Knotted Midge, a fly with two hackles, which may suggest the male and female in the paired state, and either this or a small hackle fly of the Black Spider type might be the best bet for those who do not tie their own flies.

August 1966   *C F Walker*

Realism in the nymph

Nymphal representations, from the sparse suggestive dressings of the North Country to the more sophisticated patterns of the chalk-streams, have all accounted for their fair share of trout.

The dressing method that I put before you must not be thought to be superior in any way to those patterns that have gone before. Rather, it is an exercise in manipulating fly-dressing materials and a possible striving for a more realistic approach.

The pleasure such a dressing can give is found mainly at the fly-tying bench, but when a trout is taken on such a creation—and I assure you that many trout have taken this style of nymph—then one is forced to ponder on the possible advantages of a more exact type of representation.

The pattern described was based on the mayfly nymph, but colour and material variations can be easily substituted for other species.

Tying silk is wound down the hook-shank where three fibres of cock pheasant centre tail are caught in. Also tie in a length of white acetate plastic floss and take the silk back to the head (Fig 1).

Wind the plastic floss to the shape of the natural nymph body, the abdomen and thorax being pronounced (Fig 2). Drench the floss in plastic solvent. It will then become pliable. With the fingers, manipulate the floss into the true nymphal shape, aiming for a

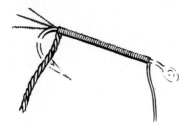

Fig 1

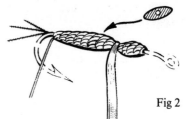

Fig 2

Fig 3

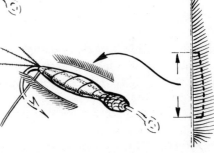

Fig 4

Fig 5

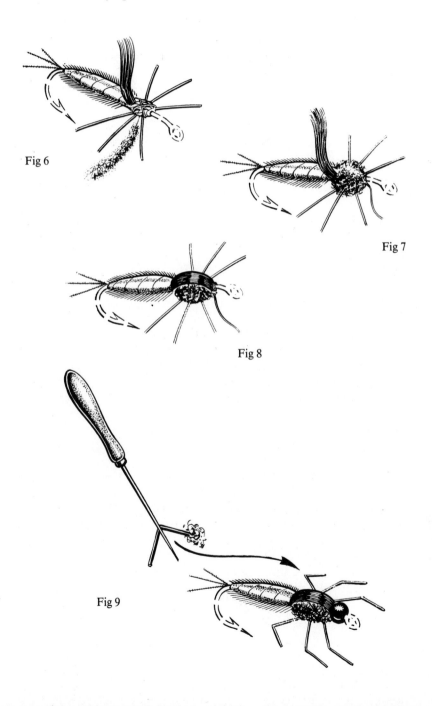

Fig 6

Fig 7

Fig 8

Fig 9

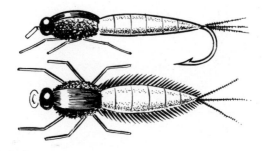

Fig 10

slightly flattened body, the amount of flatness depending upon the species.

Tie in a length of yellowish PVC surgical dressing at the point between the abdomen and the thorax. Wind the silk to the tail (Fig 3). Wind the PVC in even turns to the tail, and back again to the original starting point. Tie in with a separate length of tying silk.

Take two cock hackles. Draw the fibres down at right angles to the stem and cut back the fibres, leaving approximately 1mm (Fig 4). Cut out two pieces of the hackle to the same length as the body. Cover the PVC with clear varnish and place each portion of hackle on either side to simulate the gills. When the varnish is almost dry, work the tying silk in open turns from the tail through the shortened hackle fibres, being careful not to trap any. Secure at the neck between body and thorax.

Tie in the material to be used for the wing cases—pheasant tail or buff condor herls—and secure (Fig 5).

Take the hook from the vice and reverse it so that you can work on the underside (Fig 6). Place three lengths of nylon thread of the appropriate colour star fashion under the hook-shank and secure with figure-of-eight turns. Do not cut the legs to the correct length at this stage.

Dub the tying silk with fur from the hare's ear and proceed to wind on the thorax, making it quite prominent (Fig 7). Ensure that it is worked carefully between the legs.

Bring the wing case material over the thorax and tie in (Fig 8).

Finish off the head, making it a most prominent ball shape (Fig 9).

Varnish well. The joints in the legs must now be made. These are quite easily set by touching the correct position with the point of a heated dubbing needle. The heat causes the thread to contract and bend round the needle, creating a permanent angle. The length of the legs is now adjusted, preferably by the use of a cigarette end. This leaves a small bump on the nylon. While the leg joints remain set, the rest of the nylon leg is free to move with the water flow.

This drawing shows the finished nymph pattern and the overall effect to aim for (Fig 10).

I do not claim that such dressings will take more trout than the generally accepted patterns. However, they are a most interesting exercise in the craft of fly-dressing ... and would seem to be attractive to the fish.

September 1972 *Donald Overfield*

Flies that Kelson gave us

One of my most cherished possessions is a book called *The Salmon Fly: How To Dress It and How to Use It*, by George M Kelson, published in 1895. It was given to me, some forty years ago, by Alex Sinclair, of revered memory, who was then my father's gillie and who taught me much of what I think I know about salmon fishing and salmon flies.

The Salmon Fly is one of those delightful Victorian books that begins and ends with a section of advertisements. It is mouth-watering in these days of rising prices to see advertised 'The Springfield Boot (Patented), highly approved by HRH The Prince of Wales, black or brown cowhide, 53s 6d', or 'Real whaleskin shooting boots, hand made, the best boot possible to make, at 31s 9d'. J Peek & Son, Wholesale, Retail and Export Fishing Rod and Tackle Manufacturers, of 40 Gray's Inn Road, nineteen doors from Holborn, offer salmon flies at from 4d to 1s 6d each, and best greenheart salmon rods, 16, 17 and 18 feet, at 30s!

With flies and tackle obtainable so cheaply one wonders why it was necessary to teach people how to do-it-themselves; but the preface supplies the answer. The book was published 'by request' and was 'designed to stamp out the fallacy that no one can learn how to make a fly from written instructions'. If, as seems likely, this was really the first attempt to write a book for the do-it-yourself fly-tyer, then modern fly anglers may well owe a considerable debt of gratitude to Mr Kelson. I certainly owe him my heartfelt thanks; for I taught myself to tie flies from his book, and I still read it with pleasure for the little gems of knowledge and the fascinating glimpses of angling history that it contains.

One hundred and seventeen pages are devoted to recipes for tying about 300 different varieties of fly, and even then Mr Kelson finds time to regret the absence of a few old patterns from his list. 'No end of old time standards,' he says, 'have sunk into desuetude, disappeared from the scene and vanished altogether.' I am afraid this process still continues. I wonder how many will know Blue-over-Black by this or its earlier name? Kelson tells us that this fly was invented in the 1840s for the Usk. Apparently it was originally called William Bass after a bass singer and chimney sweeper then residing at Sevenoaks. He describes it as a capital fly in dirty water—which I readily believe—and in case anyone would like to try it, here is the recipe:

Tag Silver twist and pink silk

Tail Red toucan, yellow macaw, powdered blue macaw and gallina, in strands

Body Two turns scarlet silk and black seal's fur

Ribs Silver tinsel and silver lace

Hackle A white coch y bonddu dyed dark blue, from second turn

Wings Two strips turkey showing white tips, golden pheasant tail and peacock herl mixed together in strands, and mallard

Sides Teal.

Anyone coming to the Thurso from the end of March to the beginning of May and wanting something in the larger sizes in case of a spate and heavy water could do a lot worse than tie himself up some of these. I'll bet they would catch fish!

It is a pity that so many old patterns have become lost completely. Two, for instance, that are mentioned in the book as being old Thurso patterns, the Britannia and the Colonel, are, I am sure, not known at all to 99 per cent of modern Thurso anglers. Indeed, I think a lot of the fun has gone out of fly angling with the introduction of Waddingtons and tubes, and the supplanting of beautiful and exotic feathers, tinsels and silks by a bunch of dirty old moth-eaten hair.

Mind you, the logic behind the hairy fly is quite valid; but I maintain that you don't have to make it dull and dingy to be effective. The logic is to produce a lightly dressed, active fly that will seem alive in all conditions of water. Once when I was laid up with a bad attack of 'flu, having tired of 'whodunits', I asked for my fly-tying materials and set out to tie a series of flies with the characteristics of the hairy flies but using traditional materials. They are really what Kelson would have called grubs, and I have found them extremely effective, especially in low-water conditions and in the smaller sizes from August to the end of the season. I give you the recipes for two of them so that you can try them for yourselves. I do not think you will be disappointed.

The lochdu

Tail Some strands of black and white guinea fowl

Body Silver tinsel, oval

Hackle Black cock's hackle from the tail to the head

Throat (or wing—call it what you will) Two or three turns of black and white guinea fowl wound round and round at the head of the fly.

Tarantula

Tag Silver tinsel, oval

Tail A few strands of black and white guinea fowl

Body Pale grey darning wool

Ribs Silver tinsel, oval

Hackle Cock's hackle dyed pale blue

Throat Two or three turns of mallard, the greyish feather.

I always split my hackle feathers and the feathers that I wind on as throats, because this produces a lighter dressing.

I hope you have fun trying out these recipes, as much fun tying them as you will have in catching fish on them, and as much fun as I had in working them out.

February 1974 *Viscount Thurso*

My midge pattern has killed quality fish

Often in the warmer, calmer days of summer, trout on many stillwaters become preoccupied during the afternoons or early evenings in feeding on small midge pupae or the emerging adult in the surface film. When the trout are so engaged, the rise form is quite distinctive and can best be described as a rapid and repeated head-and-dorsal rise with the head and fin barely breaking the surface as they swim along sipping down the insects. Should there be a breeze, with a nice ripple on the water, the trout will often be observed rising and moving quite rapidly upwind in a more or less straight line. During conditions of flat calm, however, they tend to rise in a semi-circular pattern, constantly changing direction.

Among the most common of the Chironomidae (midges) that are most likely to be responsible for this rise-form are the Blagdon green midge, *Endochironomus albipennis*, the small brown midge, *Glyptotendipes paripes*, or the small red midge, *Microtendipes pedellus*. All of these are fairly small, the adults having a wing length of $\frac{1}{4}$in or less, while the pupae require a size 16 or 17 hook to represent them accurately. To use such small hooks on relatively large reservoir trout will inevitably result in a lot of fish throwing the hook. It is therefore necessary to compromise a little and use size 14 to 16 hooks.

These small midges seem to rise to the surface and hatch out fairly quickly, and it is, I think, for this reason that the trout often take the pupae right in the surface film as transformation to the winged adult takes place. When they are feeding in this way it is necessary to present your artificial only partly submerged, as in most cases they seem to completely ignore artificials fished even a little way below the surface.

For this style of fishing I have developed a special pattern that I call the Small Hatching Midge, and over the years this has stood me in good stead, but for those anglers who do not tie their own flies, a small Gold Ribbed Hare's Ear will often prove successful.

When trout are feeding on these small midges in the way described, they are far from easy to catch. In the first place, trout taking these hatching pupae are more likely to be encountered over deeper water than shallow and therefore it is the boat angler who will encounter them rather than the bank angler. Second, an emergence

Small hatching midge

of sufficient consequence to interest the trout usually occurs on relatively calm days, when the boat angler is at a distinct disadvantage.

Even when there is a good ripple on the water, the trout moving upwind, often in a straight line, will tend to pass either side of the boat, giving it a fairly wide berth. However, under these conditions, the angler stands a fair chance of taking a few nice fish, although it is often necessary to cast a distance to cover a rising fish. Even so, it is essential to use a light line and a fine leader. I find a 4lb point about right and usually fish one artificial only.

Accurate casting is also essential for this technique, for if one casts too far the trout will see the leader before the fly and go down. On the other hand, if you do not cast far enough to drop your fly in the estimated path of the trout, it will seldom deviate to accept it. Having presented your fly, it should be retrieved as slowly as possible, preferably with short pauses.

The other conditions under which this type of rise is even more likely to take place are during flat calms, and under these circumstances, especially if it is a bright sunny day, the fishing can be extremely difficult and often frustrating. To start with, unless you keep very quiet and still, restricting all unnecessary movement, few fish will be found rising within casting distance, and even when a trout does start rising in a position where you can cover it, the disturbance caused by your fly line landing on the water is often sufficient to put the fish down.

On top of all these problems, as previously explained, at this time the trout are not rising in a predetermined path and it is, therefore, most difficult to place your artificial with any accuracy. However, it is possible to take the odd fish during this period, provided you are aware of the difficulties to be overcome.

For those anglers who dress their own flies, the tying instructions for my special pattern are as follows:

Hook D/E 14 to 16

Tying silk Brown

Body Two turns of silver Lurex round bend of hook, followed by main body of dark red, green or brown condor herl

Rib Narrow silver Lurex

Thorax Buff condor herl

Hackle Small honey cock hackle (two turns only) tied in immediately behind eye of hook.

January 1970   *John Goddard*

My dressing for the midge pupa

Midges are by far the most common insects in most lakes and reservoirs and examinations of the stomach contents of trout seldom fail to reveal at least some and often great numbers of these insects, usually at the pupa stage.

Probably because eclosion ('hatching') is rapid, the winged insect leaving the water immediately, trout are not usually keen on floating imitations of it, and as the larva lives in the bottom mud, it too is less often eaten than when in pupal form.

Consequently it is at that stage that midges may most profitably be imitated. Many different dressings have been evolved and no doubt we shall see many more. That which I give is unlikely to prove to be the last word but it has the merit of proven effectiveness combined with easy tying.

There are, of course, many species of midge, of different colours, but in the dressing I give it is necessary only to vary the colour of the floss that forms the abdomen to imitate the different kinds.

To tie the fly, commence by attaching a third of a strand of marabou floss (it is a three-strand twist and you unravel it) to the point where the thorax will meet the abdomen. Wind in close turns

Red and black midge pupa

towards the hook-bend, tying in a bunch of long white or cream cock hackles as you do, in such a way that their butts project well beyond the eye and their tips beyond the bend.

When the floss has reached about a third of the way round the bend, tie in the thin end of a white cock hackle stalk. Then wind the floss back to where it commenced and there attach a length of black tying silk, which is used to tie in the end of the floss and the hackle stalk rib which is wound over the floss in an opposite spiral. Now tie in a bunch of four or five strands of any dark feather fibre with a prominent flue, carry the silk on to just behind the eye, and then twist the strands of feather fibre rope-wise and wind on to form the thorax. Tie in, cut off waste, and then whip-finish in front of the projecting butts of the cock hackle fibres, finally clipping these short at both head and tail.

The only variation for colour that does not follow the same procedure is a red one, in which the abdomen is of crimson-dyed feather fibre, lapped over with silver Lurex to leave narrow spaces between laps, through which the crimson feather fibre shows.

The method of fishing is usually to grease the leader right up to the fly and fish very slowly indeed, but sometimes better results come from leaving a yard of leader ungreased, allowing the fly half a minute to sink and then drawing it up quite quickly, repeating until the retrieve is finished.

Size should be chosen to match naturals, from No.10 to No.16.

October 1969   *Richard Walker*

The damsel and the dragon

In those hot days of summer, when the sun beats down on the water reflecting the heat into our faces, when nothing hatches and no fish stir, when perspiration stings the eye and even the noisy coots yawn in the reeds, fishing can seem to be a form of torture devised by some cunning Oriental.

We anglers perspire the day away in hot despair, hoping for the cool of the evening and for a hatch of fly that probably won't come. For those of us foolish enough to continue to fish in such conditions (and from what I have seen, this means most of us) the problem of what fly to use is ever-present, and in such circumstances even the purist is tempted to use—dare I say it?—a lure. Well, there are a couple of artificials that can perform almost miracles, and they are flies tied to represent the larvae of the damsel- and dragonflies.

In this country we are blessed with more than forty different species of the family Odonata. They are, incidentally, one of the oldest insect groups, dating back some 350 million years. A fossil from this time had a wingspan of 3ft. The mind boggles! Can you imagine what the larva looked like? Today they are more of a size we can cope with, even though many people still think they sting and seem to go in fear of them.

In the main they are creatures of smaller waters and it is on such waters that the artificial nymphs are most successful. From time to time the adult insect is taken by trout, but it is the nymph that is most attractive to the fish—and it is easier to tie.

The larvae of both groups stalk their prey with primitive stealth, shooting out their masks (articulated jaws which tuck away neatly beneath the head when not in use) to catch their food—shrimps, caddis, even tadpoles and small fish. As for the artificials, both

Dragonfly nymph

Damsel fly nymph

should be worked slowly on or near the bottom, even though the naturals themselves can put on a fair turn of speed when disturbed or when they, in turn, are hunted.

Of the two dressings, I use, that for the damsel nymph—the commoner of the two—is based on one of Richard Walker's patterns, one that has proved a killer on many waters, not least Damerham. The dragonfly larva pattern is one of my own devising, and again a proved dressing.

Both patterns can be weighted with copper or lead wire, and both can be improved by the introduction of small amounts of DFM material to the body dubbing.

Here are the dressings:

The damsel nymph
Hook Long-shanked size 8–10
Tying silk Yellow
Tail Olive hackle fibres
Body Seal's fur dyed olive with a small amount of orange worked in
Rib Yellow silk
Hackle Speckled duck or grey partridge dyed olive.

The dragonfly nymph
Hook Long-shanked size 8–10
Tying silk Black
Tail Two spikey goose quill fibres dyed olive
Body Mixed brown and olive wool, brown predominating
Rib Yellow silk
Hackle Brown partridge
Head Peacock herl.

Well, there you are—two flies that could change a day of fishing purgatory into one of success, even though the sun still beats down, the water remains as a silver mirror, perspiration stings the eyes, and the beer in your can is warm and flat.

May 1976   *Taff Price*

Those other flies . . .

Not every fly fisherman is an expert entomologist, but over the years, many of us have managed to glean a rough working knowledge of the subject. We are, for example, fascinated by the Ephemeroptera—particularly that most showy and obvious example, the mayfly (and hardly less, perhaps, by its even more useful relative the blue-winged olive). Some of us refer pontifically to our old friend the large dark olive as *Baëtis rhodani*; to the sedges as Trichoptera, to the alders as Megaloptera—and so on. It can be quite impressive.

We may not tie better imitations as a result of this apparent familiarity (and our pronunciation would probably raise a few scientific eyebrows), but the fact remains that a reasonable working knowledge of the genus and habits of the flies of stream and lake can be a useful asset to the serious fisherman. Ever since Dame Juliana Berners recommended that hackle of 'roddy wull', fishermen have been obsessed by flies—but what about all the legions of flies that are apparently obsessed by fishermen?

For some inexplicable reason I am one of those people by whom every variety of fly seems to be fascinated. I cannot think that this is due to some unmentionable reason that even my best friends would hesitate to tell me about, but whatever the reason, by any river or lake I am readily identifiable from a distance as the central core of a whirling cloud of winged insects that clearly regard me as a heaven-sent riparian blood-donor.

More than once I have been forced to abandon the field and to retreat, punctured and itching, to the shelter of my car, there to survey the baffled attackers vainly assaulting the closed windows. It is at such times particularly that I am given to wonder why we spend so much time thinking about flies that may be acceptable to the fish and so little about those that plainly find the fisherman irresistible!

Nearly all these flying, biting, blood-thirsty nuisances are what are (laughably) called 'true' flies, or Diptera. In Britain alone nearly 5,000 species have been recorded—and a terrifying study they are.

The next time you swat a mosquito on your ear or flatten a gnat on your neck you may well be reducing (infinitesimally, alas) the order of Culicidae or even Ceratopogonidae, neither of which should, of course, be confused with the non-biting midges, which (as every schoolboy knows) belong to the Chironomidae.

Then there are those particularly evil and persistent pests variously anathematised as horse flies, gad flies and clegs, none of which is likely to be less voracious if correctly addressed as Tabanidae—though to be able to identify one's enemy is (possibly) something. The list is, of course, endless: fungus gnats, fever flies, stiletto flies, robber flies, assassin flies, hover flies and hundreds more—all dignified by unpronounceable Latin names and all determined, in one way or another, to harass the genus *Homo sapiens piscatoris* without mercy.

Not that the battle is entirely one-sided. Apart from the customary manual reprisals, various protective creams and repellants are available. I have tried most of them and found some quite effective—temporarily. But for me, the cure (if you can call it that) is generally worse than the complaint. To fish smeared with some evil-smelling unguent is to put too high a price on even total immunity.

> Far better, I think,
> The sting than the stink!

There is, too, plenty of advice for the victim. Tobacco smoke is certainly a proved deterrent, and the chain-smoker coughing his way from pool to pool may well be relatively fly-free—but the price can be high, both medically and economically. In those lush southern valleys where the mosquitoes 'come not as single spies, but in battalions', I know of fishermen who ply their skilful craft in headgear draped at the back (like members of the French Foreign Legion) with handkerchiefs steeped in ammonia. Alas, they can be spoken to only in a stiff following wind. I would rather be irritated than ostracised.

Another school of thought relies on 'colour', and a gentleman in Scotland once assured me solemnly that flies 'detest blue'. Perhaps so, but not all of us are prepared to fish all summer wearing a sort of sky-blue Balaclava helmet and matching mittens! In Yorkshire, the 'sprig-of-mint' school has its adherents, and a small bunch stuck in the cap over each ear is supposed to act like a charm.

Unfortunately, my attendant dipterans don't seem to have heard about these magical properties. Nor have I forgotten the occasion when I dropped in at the local on the way home, still festooned with this particular greenery. The landlord (betraying a hitherto unexpected familiarity with the classics) enquired loudly, 'What'll it be, Bacchus?'

Frankly, I am baffled. I have tried everything. My haversack bulges with tubes, bottles, sprays and atomisers. I smoke, I calculate, approximately five fags per fish (interspersed, in particularly fly-ridden areas, with a pipe charged with a particularly noxious mixture). I exude a powerful odour of carbolic soap as a result of pre-piscatorial bathings. I have camouflaged my more vulnerable parts with a variety of sweet scented herbs, I have peered through beekeepers gauze and fumbled in muslin mittens—but all to no avail. Still they come (as the hymn says) 'in clouds descending'.

Surely it is high time that our scientists abandoned their researches into the obliteration of comparatively minor predators like the cabbage root fly, the onion fly and the lesser boll weevil. Let them focus their microscopes on what the poet once called:

Those midgets, gnats, those bugs, those flies.
That swatted wasp that never dies.

Fame, fortune and gratitude await the inventor of some odour-less greaseless, unobtrusive, concentrated and infallible fly repellant—but meanwhile the apostles of the artificial must, it seems, endure the natural as best they can.

There was an old music-hall ditty that used to ask, rather plaintively, 'Where do flies go in the winter time?' I never knew the answer to that, but I can assert, positively, where a great many of them congregate between April and October!

December 1971   *Mark Bevan*

The origin of the Muddler Minnow

The continued success of the Muddler Minnow and the construction of the unique head of this pattern, makes it necessary once again to attempt to impart the details of the technique so that this particular bogey can be laid once and for all. This is even more important now that so many variations of the Muddler are being evolved.

I first saw the original Muddler in the *Practical Fly-Fisherman* by A J McClane in 1953. McClane is the fishing editor of the US magazine *Field and Stream* and it was his experiments with this fly that brought it to the notice of the trout and bass fishermen of North America. Further information was imparted by Joseph D Bates Jr in his *Streamer Fly Tying and Fishing*, which in my opinion is the most informative and comprehensive book on streamer and hair-wing flies ever published.

The Muddler was originated on the Nipigon River in Northern Ontario by Don Gapen of the Gapen Fly Company, and was developed to imitate the Cockatush minnow found in the Nipigon and other streams in the area. So successful was the Muddler, probably because of its unique appearance, that it was tried out in other sizes to imitate other species.

In the smaller sizes, fished slowly it represented a nymph very well, and used as a floater it took fish during the grasshopper season. That it will take fish under all sorts of conditions in this part of the world as well has been proved during the last three or four seasons, and there is no sign that its popularity or success is on the wane.

The first variation of this fly was also made by Don Gapen and he called it The Thief, and since then other variations have become so

Muddler Minnow

numerous that they now merit new names and specific lists of their dressings. Richard Walker gave me a comprehensive selection for inclusion in *Reservoir and Lake Flies*, with such names as Black Muddler, Black and White Muddler, and Texas Rose Muddler, and I have even seen ingenious concoctions such as Peter Ross Muddler, Butcher Muddler and others whose names make them self-explanatory.

The success of the Muddler and the knowledge of its fish-taking qualities began to reach Great Britain in the late 1950s, and the many hundreds of requests I have had on how to construct the head started to come in about this time also. Fortunately I had had experience with the particular technique involved, as it is the same one used in the construction of the hair-bodied flies that are popular in the United States for freshwater bass fishing. They were evolved for their floating qualities and because this particular type of body can be trimmed into shape after application so that it is possible to make lures representing frogs, mice, shrews, etc, which can be realistically reproduced and which can be worked across the surface of the water in a most lifelike manner.

The material used is the body hair of the deer, and as this varies in colour from a deep brown through grey to a pale buff, some colour variations, including barred effects, may be made without dyeing.

I emphasise that it is the body hair that must be used because of the texture of these hairs, which not only enables the lure to float when necessary but also makes possible the particular method of application. This is because the individual hairs are stiff and quite thick, and finer hairs such as those from the tail will not spin round the hook shank as we need them to.

The actual method of application is simple and requires little practice. I think it presents a problem only in so far that the technique is less well known than putting on wings and dubbing bodies and other fly-tying procedures more universally known, particularly in Great Britain. I will kill two birds with one stone and give the details of making a complete hair body, the only difference as far as the Muddler is concerned being that the procedure is carried out at the head of the fly only.

Place the hook (usually a long shanked one for Muddlers) in the vice and fix the tying silk at the bend of the hook. No silk is wound round that part of the hook where the hair is to be applied.

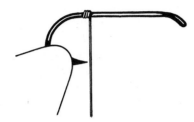

Fig 11

Fig 12

Fig 13

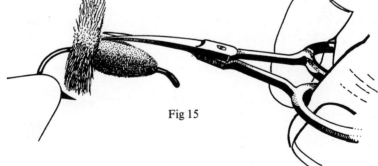

Fig 14

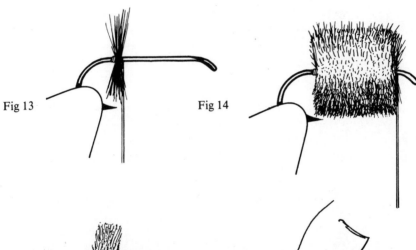

Fig 15

Cut a small bunch of the body hairs from the skin and hold them over the hook immediately above where the silk is tied in, and in line with the shank (Fig 11).

Now take two loose turns round the fur and the hook shank just firm enough to hold the fur on to the hook so that the fingers may be released (Fig 12). Exactly at the same time as the fingers are released, the silk is pulled tight and the hairs will flare round the hook shank to make a hackle effect, as in Fig 13. In other words, this action is a complete negation of all we have ever learned with regard to putting on wings and tails, when everything is held firmly between the fingers and brought down by the silk on to the top of the hook.

The silk should now be behind the 'hackle' at this stage, so still keeping it tight, pass it through the 'hackle', make a half-hitch round the hook shank in front of it and press it close back up to the 'hackle'. The procedure is now repeated with another bunch of hairs and another half-hitch as before. Carry on until the necessary amount of hook-shank has been covered, and the result should be a 'flue-brush' anything from 1in to $1\frac{1}{2}$in in diameter (Fig 14).

The 'brush' is then trimmed to shape, using a sharp pair of scissors (Fig 15), curved blades making a neater cut than straight ones, and the result is a bristle body not necessarily of the shape shown in Fig 15, as tapered and other silhouettes can be imparted.

Exactly the same method is used for making the head of all the Muddlers, but in this case the hairs are applied after the rest of the fly has been constructed.

A fairly stout tying silk should be used so that the turns of silk can be pulled really tight, and at this stage I would like to mention an idea given to me by Geoffrey Bucknall and others, to ensure that the hairs remain fixed for the lifetime of the fly. This entails applying a clear polyurethane varnish to the roots of the hairs after each 'hackle' has been formed and the half-hitch of silk pushed up to it. The point of a dubbing needle is dipped into the varnish and the resulting droplet applied to the half-hitch and the roots of the hairs. The varnish sets rock-hard, and MM heads I have constructed and 'fixed' in this manner have proved to be immovable, no matter how harshly they are treated.

May 1970   *John Veniard*

New ways with salmon flies

Donald Downs and I were caught up in the present trend to re-introduce classic angling books of the past when we were asked to contribute a new section to Dr T E Pryce-Tannatt's *How to Dress Salmon Flies*. We had the good fortune to enlist the help of Mr Freddie Riley, who has gone to great lengths to produce exotic salmon flies equal to any made in the past and has also devised some new tying techniques.

This enthusiasm for the angling classics is a healthy sign. Not only does it give the present generation of young anglers the chance to study the works of those who laid the foundations of modern fly fishing, but it also gives them the opportunity to see for themselves the painstaking efforts that went into their experiments and observations.

Many young anglers today probably think that most of the flies they use and the techniques of their presentation, are the result of contemporary thought. This is far from always the case. The reservoir lures they can cast such great distances today had their beginnings in the Demons and Terrors in use at the turn of the century. And it was G E M Skues, in 1910, who first saw the potential of fishing the nymph, that most popular of modern flies. Those publishers who are making possible this return to the origins of our sport deserve our thanks.

One of the biggest changes that has taken place in fly-fishing is that of the angler's approach to the artificial fly. This has been brought about by the change in his habits, in that he now considers that the fly he ties himself must be superior to the shop-bought product. This does not mean that the amateur ties a better fly than the professional fly-tyer, and, fortunately, many professional tyers are also expert anglers, so flies can still be bought with confidence. It is, however, my considered opinion that the fly has now progressed from being usually a shop-bought item of tackle to being an expression of an individual angler's interpretation of a dressing that will take fish, plus an essential part of his angling pleasure. This aspect of the fly-tying craft was not really appreciated, I feel, when Pryce-Tannatt produced his book, although the obvious beauty of the flies in the illustrations must have done much to foster interest.

I have referred to fly-tying as a 'craft' rather than as an 'art', which is its customary description. I do this deliberately because I know that fly-tying can be practised by anyone who is interested enough, whereas an artist has a special gift. That the craft can be transformed into an art form is also true, however, and I have been fortunate enough to have seen many examples where this has been the case.

There is one instance where Pryce-Tannatt makes a contribution to fostering pride in the appearance of one's flies, and that is in the section devoted to giving form and symmetry to one's efforts. This certainly prompted me to make my own flies as attractive as possible, and resulted in my tying flies that I thought were worth looking at, as well as being used to catch fish—which is where we get back to Freddie Riley . . .

One of the features that Freddie has concentrated on—in fact the main feature—is the extreme neatness and style of his flies, and nowhere is this more evident than in the bodies. So let me concentrate on this aspect of salmon fly-tying, up to the stage where the throat hackle has been tied in and wound, and the fly is ready to take its wings.

The first stage in all his patterns is the underbody of wool. This is tied in as Fig 16, wound to the point where the body will be finished off, and then back again in the manner shown in Fig 17. Each wind is a touching turn, which is essential if real symmetry is to be achieved. The turns of wool are finished at the position shown in Fig 18, immediately above the point of the hook. The tying silk is then taken to the position shown in Fig 18, and fine oval tinsel tied in for the tag.

The winding of the tag is shown in Figs 19 and 20, and the object of this method is to have the turns of tinsel wound without having either tying silk or the ends of the tinsel underneath them. This results in a flat tag, with absolutely no distortion.

The silk for the rest of the tag is tied in and wound as in Fig 21, ensuring that it tightly covers the two ends of the tinsel. Now the tail is tied in, as is the ostrich herl for the butt. All this is taking place in the space left at the end of the wool body.

The next step is to wind the butt and to ensure that a close ruff is achieved, as in the illustration. This is done by winding to the right, ensuring that the flue is on the left-hand side of its quill, not the right. A little experimentation will soon enlighten you as to the reason for this, if you do not know it already.

Now the oval tinsel for the rib is tied in, followed by the floss silk

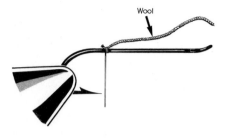

Wool

Fig 16

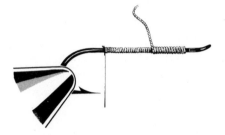

Fig 17

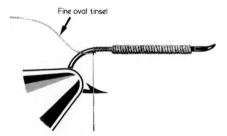

Fine oval tinsel

Fig 18

Enlarged views of the tag

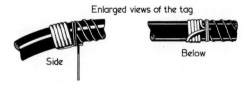

Side

Below

Fig 19 Fig 20

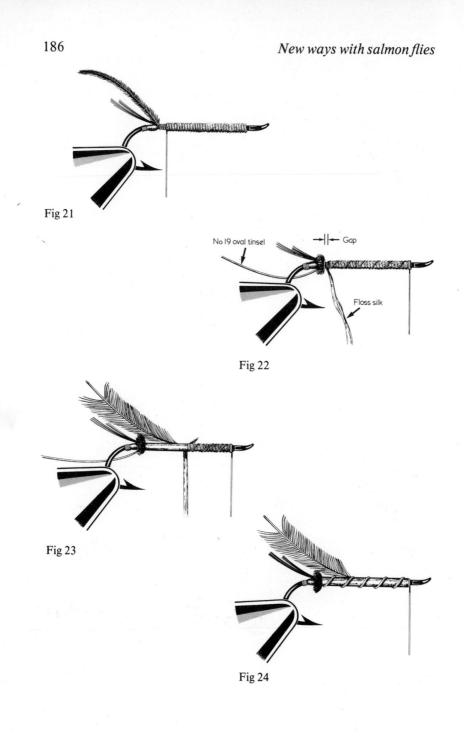

Fig 21

Fig 22

No 19 oval tinsel

Gap

Floss silk

Fig 23

Fig 24

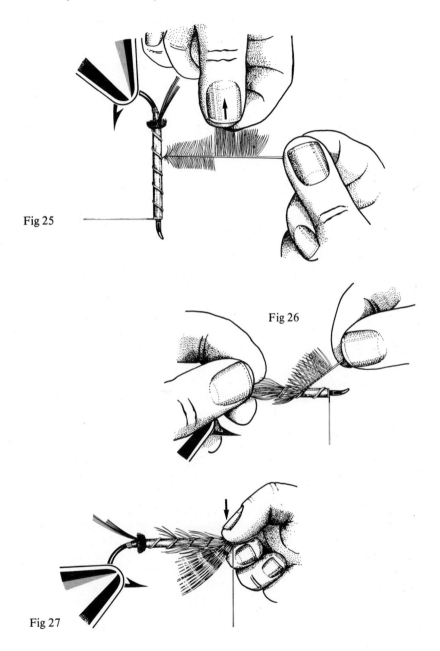

Fig 25

Fig 26

Fig 27

for the body, and we are still within the space left at the end (Fig 22). Take the tying silk back to the front of the body, as shown in this drawing. Although this shows the silk as a rib, this is only for clarity of illustration. It actually sinks into the wool underbody.

Turns of the body floss are now wound in the remainder of the gap, and then, when the floss is level with the wool underbody, it is wound up to the stage shown in Fig 23, where the body hackle is tied in. It will be seen that the whole of the rear part of the fly, from the back-end of the tag through to the point where the hackle is tied in, is one smooth whole, with no indication where any items were tied in or finished off. This is the whole object of the exercise.

The floss silk is now wound down the rest of the body, continuing the smooth silhouette, followed by turns of the evenly-wound tinsel rib (Fig 24). Freddie prefers to use a rayon floss for his bodies to achieve the ultimate in smoothness, and it works. Although narrower than some of the real silks we use, it tends to spread while being wound and lies absolutely flat. Unless one is very careful, real silk can tend to 'rope'.

Unlike some of us, Freddie ties in his body hackles undoubled, preferring to double them after they are tied in as shown in Fig 25.

Once the hackle has been doubled, it is wound to the front of the body, the quill being pressed firmly against the oval ribbing tinsel, while the hackle fibres are stroked to the rear (Fig 26). Both these actions ensure that the hackles will have the attractive backward sweep that is the hallmark of a well-wound body hackle. Any surplus body hackle is cut off after one complete turn has been made at the front.

The throat hackle now has to be tied in and wound (no false hackles here), and this can either be doubled, as shown in Fig 25, or before it is tied in. When this has been completed, firm pressure with the thumb and forefinger is applied (Fig 27). This ensures that the fibres are evenly separated, ready for the wings to be added.

There is no reason why this method of making salmon fly bodies should not be applied to our trout flies, particularly those tied on long-shanked hooks.

January 1975   *John Veniard*

Dry-fly conversions

It seems strange to me that we lack the principle of the general 'attractor' dry fly, equivalent to those wet-fly patterns that copy nothing in particular. The whole concept of the dry fly is that it should be entirely imitative, perhaps because its modern development was so strongly influenced by the chalk-stream philosophy. The only exception would appear to be the dry Wickham and the Pink Wickham, though even these were firmly established on the Test before Halford and Skues, and they grudgingly accepted them, trying to fit them in to some sort of relationship with the natural insect.

I began to think on different lines last year when I was fishing a single bright Woodcock and Yellow as a wet fly. It persistently refused to sink. Then I cast it to a trout moving upwind on the left-hand side of my boat. The fly landed in its path, floated on its side and was immediately snaffled by the trout. I recollected the story of an American who used a scarlet fanwing on the Test with huge success. My own yellow fly was really garish, with a bright, fluorescent body and hackle, and a tippet tail.

By the end of June I felt really jaded with normal wet-fly fishing. The trout were easy enough to catch and, in these days of intensive stocking, far from critical. In the heat of the day a deeply worked lure would invariably take fish from the bottom, or near it, but it seemed a sad way to catch fish, so I confined myself to evening dry-fly sessions with special patterns.

What I did was to take three patterns of fly that are highly successful as sunk patterns, but are never tied as floaters—at least not according to my comprehensive library—and tied them as dry flies. The conversion is simple enough, mostly being of a collar of stiff cock's hackle equivalent to the wet one of hen. The chosen flies were Invicta, Mallard and Claret, and Butcher.

In fact the Invicta turned out to be an imitative fly by accident, for, tied as a floater, it was killing during sedge hatches. I've always known that the Invicta is one of the most effective flies to fish just below the surface when sedges are hatching, but as a floater it bears little resemblance to the natural sedge and I would normally use a dry Cinnamon or Little Red Sedge in those conditions.

A dry Invicta has a bright yellow body, ribbed with gold, and tail whisks of golden pheasant topping. For buoyancy I wound on a palmer body of natural red-game cock, tied in another at the throat with a grizzle hackle dyed bright blue in front. The hen-pheasant wing was tied on flat in the usual dry-sedge style. This fly was a real killer when sedges were active in the evening.

The best way to fish the dry Invicta was to cast it to rising trout as they were knocking off sedges on the surface. From a boat, I found it best to angle the fly across-wind to fish moving up through the ripple, so that the trout came to it when it was riding with no drag from line or wind. I had many limit bags at Sundridge to this fly on warm, summer evenings. A size 12 proved just right.

The normal wet Mallard and Claret is a mystery fly in the sense that it kills at times when it proves impossible to relate it to any particular insect. The best I can do is to relate it to isolated buzzer hatches on lakes, especially when darkish buzzers are coming away sporadically in the afternoon, but this is hardly good enough, because this wet fly definitely kills fish when they are rising to almost any natural fly. The theory is that it suggests a non-specific nymph rising to the surface and, although it kills at any depth, it proves most effective fished just below the surface. This is why I made this into a floater with a stiff claret-dyed cock hackle, the fly dressing being otherwise the same as for the standard wet fly.

The story here was different from that of the Invicta, for although it failed to score notably in sedge hatches, it brought fish up in bright daylight when there was no other surface activity. On two occasions there was a scattered late-afternoon rise on the lake, which I attributed to a small, dark buzzer, although there were no discernible fly moving off the water. On both these occasions the dry Mallard and Claret killed two fish, rising many more. I would be happy to fish this fly along the oily wind-lanes you find on large reservoirs when you see trout taking small black gnats sticking in the surface films.

The last shot in the locker is the dry Butcher, which, I seem to remember, had a short vogue when I was quite young. I have not heard of its application for many years and I imagine it was then a passing fad. What I was after was a tiny, glittering morsel, shining in the sunlight, for all the world like a newly-hatched fly drying the moisture from its wings. It was used with mixed success but persistently refused to bring up fish in flat calms, although fished in a bright, sunlit ripple, it produced swirls as well as firm takes.

It is best to omit the blue mallard wings unless you really want to split them and set them upright. The red tail, the silver body and a stiff, black cock's hackle are the basic requirements. Of course, the usual Butcher variants can also be tied—a golden-bodied one, another with scarlet hackle for the Bloody Butcher, or orange hackle with blue tail for the Kingfisher version. They all work well.

There seems no reason why you shouldn't convert any favourite wet-fly pattern to a floater, but what is interesting is that it's not just the fly pattern that succeeds but the philosophy of a general attractor fly as well. Is there any reason why a trout should be more critical of a wet fly than a dry? Of course not. Nor is there any reason why the most effective wet flies should fail as floaters—and in practice they do not.

May 1976   *Geoffrey Bucknall*

Just a little bit of red

I have never been quite satisfied with my own or anybody else's tyings of mayfly duns and spinners.

Before the last war, when I relied on bought flies, I found that the all-hackle Straddlebug pattern was attractive to the trout on the Irish loughs. In fact, during a hatch of duns the fish seemed to prefer them to the natural, but they were not good floaters and as they fished best when riding high on the water they had to be constantly dried and re-greased.

The problem seemed to me to be how best to produce the correct size of both body and wings without making a bulky and heavy finished article. In addition, I wanted to incorporate two features that experience has taught me to be desirable.

First, I have never been able to detect any trace of red in a mayfly dun, but I am convinced that a little red in the front hackle pays dividends. Second, at times, during a fall of spinner, the fish, for some reason known only to themselves, will look only at flies that are completely spent and lying flat on the surface film.

I have been amusing myself this winter tying bodies of feather-fibre. All my capes finish up with a lot of beautiful but quite useless feathers about 4in long. I take one of these (Rhode Island Red for the dun and black Andalusian for the spinner) and cut off the fibres to within about ⅛in from the central stalk. Then I tie in the tip at the bend and wind it up the shank towards the eye in close turns, give it a whip finish, cut off the surplus stalk, remove it from the vice and trim up the body to a nice tapered shape.

Before doing this, I tie in a fine-pointed hackle tail (red for the dun and black for the spinner) and form a base for the body with floss silk (light yellow for the dun and white for the spinner).

For the dun I use two white hackles, the first dyed red and the front one dyed pale green. I don't like using dyed feathers because I feel that the dying takes some of the nature out of the feather, but the double hackle should compensate for this.

For the spinner I use one black hackle and if I want it to lie flat I spread out the fibres horizontally on either side and finish with a figure-of-eight.

I have tied a few duns with a fine gold ribbing for use in bright sunshine, but this adds weight and should not be necessary on dull days.

March 1972   *Stanley Woodrow*